Why Some Men Might Tolerate Infidelity

Understanding the Psychology Behind Accepting Infidelity

A.A. CASTOR

Table of Contents

Why Some Men Might Tolerate Infidelity: Understanding the Psychology Behind Accepting Infidelity

A.A. CASTOR

Philippine Copyright Law:

The Intellectual Property Code of the Philippines (Republic Act No. 8293) provides protection to literary and artistic works from the moment of their creation. It includes provisions for the rights of authors and copyright owners, including the exclusive right to reproduce, distribute, perform, and display their works. Unauthorized use or reproduction of copyrighted materials is subject to legal penalties under this law.

Dedication

To my beloved family,

Your unconditional love, unwavering support, and endless encouragement have been my greatest blessings. From the earliest days of dreaming to the challenging moments of writing, you have stood by me with patience and belief. This book is as much yours as it is mine, a reflection of the values you've instilled and the faith you've shown in me. Thank you for being my rock and my inspiration.

To my dear friends,

Your friendship has illuminated my path with laughter, shared moments, and invaluable support. You've cheered me on through every triumph and lifted me up through every challenge. Your belief in my endeavors has been a source of strength and motivation. This book is a testament to the power of friendship, and I am grateful for each of you who has walked this journey by my side.

To God,

Your grace and guidance have been my constant companions. In moments of doubt, you've shown me the way; in moments of joy, you've multiplied my gratitude. This book is a testament to your faithfulness and the blessings you've bestowed upon me. May it serve as a reflection of your love and the lessons you continue to teach me.

With heartfelt gratitude and love,

A.A. Castor

Why I Am Writing This Book

Infidelity is often seen as one of the greatest threats to a romantic relationship, leading to feelings of betrayal, heartbreak, and the end of partnerships. However, there are instances where some men not only tolerate but also accept infidelity from their partners. This phenomenon challenges conventional wisdom about love, fidelity, and relationship dynamics, raising important questions about human psychology and emotional resilience.

In writing "Why Some Men Might Tolerate Infidelity: Understanding the Psychology Behind Accepting Infidelity," I aim to explore the complex and multifaceted reasons behind this acceptance. This book is the culmination of years of research, conversations, and personal observations about relationships, societal norms, and individual behaviors. It seeks to provide a comprehensive understanding of why some men may choose to remain in relationships where infidelity occurs openly or is discovered.

Through this book, I hope to achieve several objectives:

1. **Demystify the Behavior:** By delving into the psychological, emotional, and social factors that contribute to the tolerance of infidelity, I aim to demystify this behavior. Understanding the underlying reasons can foster empathy and reduce judgment towards those who find themselves in such situations.
2. **Challenge Stereotypes:** Traditional views on relationships and fidelity are often rigid and simplistic. This book aims to challenge these stereotypes by presenting a nuanced perspective on male responses to infidelity, highlighting that each individual's reaction is influenced by a myriad of factors.
3. **Promote Healthy Dialogue:** Infidelity is a taboo topic that often leads to hushed conversations and secretive coping mechanisms. By bringing this subject into the open, I hope to encourage healthy dialogue and support for those navigating similar experiences.
4. **Provide Insights for Relationship Dynamics:** Understanding why some men tolerate infidelity can offer valuable insights for both partners in a relationship. It can help individuals recognize and address underlying issues, improve communication, and foster healthier relationship dynamics.
5. **Broaden Perspectives on Commitment and Fidelity:** This book aims to broaden perspectives on what commitment and fidelity mean in modern relationships. By examining alternative relationship structures and coping mechanisms, it provides a broader view of how love and loyalty can manifest.

Ultimately, this book is not about condoning or condemning infidelity but about understanding the human psyche and the diverse ways people navigate their intimate relationships. It is an exploration of resilience, forgiveness, societal influences, and personal boundaries. By shedding light on this often-overlooked aspect of relationship dynamics, I hope to contribute to a more compassionate and informed discourse on love and fidelity.

Warning and Disclaimer

Before delving into the contents of this book, it is essential to clarify my stance on the topic discussed. This book, "Why Some Men Might Tolerate Infidelity: Understanding the Psychology Behind Accepting Infidelity," is written with the intention of exploring and understanding the psychological and emotional factors that lead some men to accept infidelity in their relationships.

Important Notice:

- **Not an Endorsement:** In no way am I advocating for or endorsing infidelity. Infidelity can cause significant emotional pain and harm, and it is not a recommended or justified behavior.

- **Understanding, Not Justifying:** The goal of this book is to provide insights into why some men may tolerate infidelity, not to justify or excuse such actions. It is about understanding human behavior and relationship dynamics.

- **Individual Differences:** Each person's experience and reaction to infidelity are unique. This book does not intend to generalize or diminish the feelings of those who have been hurt by infidelity.

- **Seek Professional Advice:** If you are dealing with infidelity in your relationship, it is crucial to seek professional advice from a licensed therapist or counselor. This book is not a substitute for professional guidance or therapy.

- **Respect and Consent:** All relationships should be based on mutual respect, trust, and consent. Infidelity often violates these principles, and addressing such issues should involve open and honest communication between partners.

By reading this book, you agree to approach the subject with an open mind and understand that the purpose is to explore and analyze, not to promote or normalize infidelity. The insights provided are meant to foster empathy and understanding, contributing to healthier discussions and better relationship dynamics.

Thank you for your understanding.

Mr. A.A. Castor

About the Author

Mr. A.A. Castor is an accomplished researcher and author whose work is deeply rooted in the exploration of human behavior, particularly within the intricate realms of relationships and psychology. With a robust academic background in psychology and a passion for understanding the complexities of intimate connections, Mr. Castor has dedicated his career to unraveling the mysteries of human behavior and emotions.

His journey into the study of relationships began with a fascination for how individuals navigate the dynamics of love, trust, and commitment. Through years of rigorous research and personal introspection, Mr. Castor has developed a keen insight into the diverse ways people perceive and experience intimate relationships. This exploration led him to delve into less conventional topics, such as the acceptance of infidelity by some men within their relationships.

Drawing on a blend of empirical research, theoretical frameworks, and real-world observations, Mr. Castor brings a nuanced perspective to the discussion of why some men may tolerate infidelity. His approach is characterized by empathy and a deep respect for the complexities of human emotions, seeking not only to uncover the underlying psychological mechanisms but also to foster understanding and dialogue on a topic often shrouded in stigma and judgment.

Beyond his academic pursuits, Mr. Castor is committed to promoting thoughtful discourse and expanding the boundaries of knowledge in psychology and relationship studies. His writing reflects a dedication to bridging the gap between scholarly research and practical insights, offering readers a deeper understanding of the human psyche and its implications for intimate relationships.

Through his work, Mr. Castor strives to challenge traditional narratives, encourage critical thinking, and provide a compassionate lens through which to view the intricacies of human connections. His contributions aim to empower individuals to navigate their relationships with greater understanding, empathy, and authenticity.

As an author, researcher, and advocate for psychological insight, Mr. A.A. Castor continues to push the boundaries of knowledge in his field, inspiring readers to explore new perspectives and embrace the complexities of human emotions and relationships.

Introduction

In historical contexts, the concept of cuckoldry primarily refers to a husband who has been betrayed by his wife's infidelity, rather than a consensual practice agreed upon by both partners. The term "cuckold" historically carries negative connotations, depicting a man who is unaware of or humiliated by his wife's extramarital affairs. It is rooted in cultural narratives and literary traditions that often emphasize male dishonor and betrayal within marriage.

While historical texts and artworks frequently depict scenarios of cuckoldry, they typically do not document consensual arrangements where a husband willingly agrees to or derives pleasure from his wife's sexual relationships with other men. Instead, these references often serve as moral or cautionary tales, reinforcing societal norms around fidelity, marriage, and male honor.

In modern usage and within certain subcultures, "cuckoldry" or "cuckolding" has evolved to encompass consensual non-monogamous practices where all parties involved agree to the arrangement. This contemporary understanding contrasts with historical depictions, reflecting changing attitudes towards sexuality, relationships, and individual agency in the present day.

In modern times, there are individuals and couples who openly practice consensual cuckolding as part of their sexual or relationship dynamics. This practice typically involves a mutual agreement where one partner (usually the husband or male partner) derives arousal or satisfaction from their female partner engaging in sexual activities with other men. The dynamics of cuckolding can vary widely, but it often includes elements of voyeurism, submission, and compersion (taking pleasure in a partner's pleasure).

People who engage in consensual cuckolding often emphasize the importance of clear communication, trust, and mutual respect within their relationship. For them, cuckolding is not about betrayal or humiliation but rather an exploration of sexual fantasies, power dynamics, and emotional connections in a controlled and consensual manner. It can be seen as a way to enhance intimacy, trust, and understanding between partners who share similar desires and boundaries.

In contemporary discussions about sexuality and relationships, there are online communities, forums, and educational resources where individuals openly discuss their experiences with cuckolding, share advice, and seek support from like-minded individuals. This openness reflects evolving attitudes towards sexuality and the recognition of diverse relationship dynamics beyond traditional monogamous norms.

The concept of cuckoldry has a rich and complex history, dating back to ancient times. The term "cuckold" originates from the Old French word "cucu," derived from the cuckoo bird, which lays its eggs in other birds' nests, symbolizing infidelity.

Medieval and Renaissance Era

During the Medieval and Renaissance eras, cuckoldry was a prevalent motif in literature, folklore, and art, reflecting societal attitudes towards marriage, honor, and sexual fidelity. In these periods, cuckoldry symbolized a man's perceived loss of control over his wife's fidelity, often portrayed as a source of shame and humiliation for the husband.

Literary works from this time, including plays and poems, frequently featured cuckolded husbands as characters, with their stories serving as cautionary tales or moral lessons. These narratives explored themes of jealousy, betrayal, and the consequences of infidelity within the context of marriage and social norms.

William Shakespeare, in particular, incorporated themes of cuckoldry in several of his plays. In "Othello," the character of Othello becomes consumed by jealousy and suspicion due to false accusations of his wife Desdemona's infidelity, leading to tragic consequences. In "The Merry Wives of Windsor," the character of Falstaff attempts to seduce two married women, Mistress Ford and Mistress Page, but ultimately becomes a victim of their humorous and clever schemes, highlighting the comedic aspects of cuckoldry.

Artistic representations of cuckoldry in paintings and illustrations during this era often depicted scenes of marital betrayal or the discovery of infidelity, emphasizing the moral and social implications of such transgressions. These artworks contributed to the cultural narrative surrounding fidelity and honor, shaping public perceptions and discussions about relationships and morality during the Medieval and Renaissance periods.

Early Modern Period

During the Early Modern Period, which spanned roughly from the late 15th to the late 18th century, cuckoldry continued to be a prevalent theme in literature, drama, and satire. This period marked a transition from the medieval worldview to a more humanistic and individualistic outlook, influencing how cuckoldry was portrayed in artistic and literary works.

Literature and drama of the time often used cuckoldry as a tool for social commentary and satire, reflecting shifting societal attitudes towards marriage, sexuality, and gender roles. Cuckolded husbands were frequently depicted as figures of ridicule, highlighting the perceived loss of honor and control over their wives' fidelity. Plays, such as those by playwrights like Ben Jonson and John Webster, explored themes of jealousy, betrayal, and deception within the context of marriage.

Satirical pamphlets and writings also capitalized on the comedic and moralistic aspects of cuckoldry, using humor and exaggeration to critique societal norms and behaviors. These works often portrayed cuckolded husbands as naive or foolish, contrasting them with cunning and deceptive characters who orchestrated their humiliation.

Artistic representations during this period, particularly in paintings and prints, further emphasized the themes of cuckoldry through visual storytelling. Scenes of marital betrayal or the discovery of infidelity were depicted with symbolic elements that reinforced moral lessons or societal expectations around fidelity and honor.

Overall, the Early Modern Period saw cuckoldry evolve from a traditional motif of shame and dishonor to a subject of satire and social critique. Literary and artistic works of the time provided insights into changing attitudes towards marriage and relationships, reflecting broader cultural shifts towards individualism and the questioning of established norms.

19th and 20th Century

In the 19th and 20th centuries, societal attitudes towards marriage, fidelity, and sexuality underwent significant shifts, influencing how cuckoldry was perceived and portrayed in cultural discourse. During this period, cuckoldry evolved beyond its traditional association with shame and dishonor to encompass more nuanced psychological and sociological perspectives.

In literature and art, cuckoldry continued to be explored as a theme, albeit with new interpretations and contexts. Writers and artists of the 19th century began to delve deeper into the emotional and psychological dimensions of cuckoldry, examining its impact on individuals and relationships. For example, novels such as Gustave Flaubert's

"Madame Bovary" and Thomas Hardy's "Tess of the d'Urbervilles" explored themes of infidelity and marital betrayal, highlighting the complexities and consequences of straying from societal norms.

Psychologists and sociologists also began to study cuckoldry as a phenomenon with broader implications for human behavior and relationships. Sigmund Freud's theories on psychoanalysis, for instance, introduced concepts of desire, repression, and unconscious motivations that could influence marital dynamics, including infidelity. Meanwhile, sociological studies explored how cultural norms and societal expectations shaped perceptions of fidelity and the consequences of its breach.

In popular culture, cuckoldry became less of a straightforward moral trope and more of a complex psychological and social issue. While the term itself became less common in mainstream discourse, it persisted in certain subcultures and literary genres where it continued to provoke discussions about trust, betrayal, and the evolving nature of intimate relationships.

Overall, the 19th and 20th centuries marked a period of transition for cuckoldry, from a symbol of shame and dishonor to a subject of psychological inquiry and social critique. This evolution reflected broader changes in societal values, gender roles, and the understanding of human sexuality, paving the way for more nuanced explorations of fidelity and infidelity in modern discourse.

Contemporary Understanding

In contemporary times, the concept of cuckoldry has undergone significant evolution, particularly within the context of consensual non-monogamous relationships. While historically associated with shame and humiliation for a husband whose partner was unfaithful, modern interpretations of cuckoldry often take on consensual and even erotic dimensions.

One of the notable contemporary understandings of cuckoldry revolves around it being a fetish or kink. In this context, individuals or couples derive sexual arousal or gratification from the fantasy or reality of one partner engaging in sexual activity with someone else. Unlike its historical connotations, where cuckoldry was often involuntary and a source of distress, modern interpretations embrace it as a consensual form of sexual expression within the bounds of ethical non-monogamy.

This shift reflects broader societal changes in attitudes towards sexuality, intimacy, and relationship dynamics. It highlights a growing acceptance and exploration of diverse sexual fantasies and practices, where consent, communication, and mutual enjoyment are prioritized. For those who engage in consensual cuckoldry, the experience can be a way to explore trust, intimacy, and sexual boundaries in a controlled and respectful manner, contrary to the historical narratives of shame and betrayal.

Moreover, contemporary discussions around cuckoldry often intersect with broader conversations about sexual liberation, individual autonomy, and the redefinition of traditional relationship norms. As people continue to explore and define their sexual identities and desires, consensual forms of cuckoldry exemplify how personal and sexual relationships can be negotiated and understood in diverse and evolving ways in the modern era.

Psychological Perspectives

Contemporary psychology offers insightful perspectives on cuckoldry, examining it through the lenses of power dynamics, control dynamics, and emotional responses within relationships. Here's a deeper exploration of these psychological perspectives:

1. **Power Dynamics**: Cuckoldry can be seen as a manifestation of power dynamics within relationships. From

this perspective, the individual who consents to or enjoys the idea of their partner's infidelity may derive a sense of power from the situation. This power can stem from various factors, such as control over their own emotions or the relationship dynamics, and even the ability to set and negotiate boundaries.

2. **Control Dynamics**: Within consensual cuckoldry, there is often a complex interplay of control dynamics. The partner who is not directly involved in the sexual activity may exercise control over the situation by giving consent, setting rules and boundaries, or even deriving pleasure from the perceived loss of control. This can lead to a deeper exploration of personal limits, trust, and the negotiation of desires and boundaries between partners.

3. **Emotional Responses**: Individuals involved in consensual cuckoldry may experience a range of emotional responses, which contemporary psychology seeks to understand and contextualize. These responses can include arousal, jealousy, compersion (feeling joy from a partner's joy), and a heightened sense of intimacy and connection with their partner. Exploring these emotions within the framework of consensual non-monogamy allows individuals and couples to navigate complex feelings in a supportive and communicative environment.

4. **Exploration of Dominance and Submission**: For some individuals, consensual cuckoldry serves as a platform to explore themes of dominance and submission. The act of willingly allowing or participating in a partner's sexual activity with someone else can challenge traditional notions of possessiveness and exclusivity. This exploration can deepen trust and intimacy by fostering open communication and negotiation of desires and boundaries.

5. **Trust and Intimacy**: Trust is a central theme in consensual cuckoldry, as it involves a high degree of trust between partners. The willingness to share intimate fantasies and experiences, and to negotiate boundaries, requires a foundation of trust and mutual respect. For many, consensual cuckoldry can strengthen emotional bonds and enhance intimacy by encouraging vulnerability and honest communication about desires and insecurities.

In summary, contemporary psychological perspectives on cuckoldry emphasize its complexity and diversity within consensual non-monogamous relationships. By examining power dynamics, control dynamics, emotional responses, and themes of dominance and submission, psychologists seek to provide insights into how individuals navigate and understand their sexual desires, trust, and intimacy within the context of modern relationships.

Cultural Representation

Cultural representations of cuckoldry in modern media reflect a blend of historical attitudes and contemporary interpretations, shaping ongoing discussions about human sexuality and relationships. Here's a closer look at how cuckoldry is portrayed across different cultural mediums:

1. **Literature**: In literature, cuckoldry has been a recurring theme, both historically and in modern times. Works often explore the emotional and psychological dimensions of infidelity, ranging from tragedy and betrayal to comedy and satire. Authors use cuckoldry to delve into themes of trust, jealousy, and the complexities of human desire. Contemporary literature continues to challenge traditional narratives, portraying cuckoldry in consensual and non-consensual contexts, exploring its impact on characters and relationships.

2. **Film and Television**: Cuckoldry appears in various films and TV shows, reflecting societal attitudes and exploring its psychological and emotional ramifications. Whether depicted as a source of humor, drama, or eroticism, film and television portrayals often highlight the power dynamics, emotional turmoil, and relational consequences associated with infidelity. Modern interpretations may also include consensual

cuckoldry, portraying characters who explore non-traditional relationship dynamics and sexual fantasies.

3. **Online Forums and Communities**: The internet has facilitated discussions and communities centered around cuckoldry and consensual non-monogamy. Online forums provide platforms for individuals to share experiences, seek advice, and discuss fantasies in a supportive environment. These digital spaces contribute to the normalization and understanding of cuckoldry as a valid expression of sexual desire and relationship dynamics. They also reflect diverse perspectives on trust, intimacy, and personal boundaries within consensual relationships.

4. **Art and Visual Culture**: Visual representations of cuckoldry in art often explore themes of voyeurism, betrayal, and intimacy. Historical artworks depict mythological and biblical narratives, such as the stories of Venus and Mars, or biblical figures like Susanna, emphasizing moral lessons and societal norms. Contemporary artists may reinterpret these themes, using visual mediums to challenge conventions and provoke thought on relationships, sexuality, and personal autonomy.

5. **Social Commentary and Debate**: Cuckoldry continues to provoke social commentary and debate, reflecting evolving attitudes toward sexuality, gender roles, and relationship norms. Media representations offer a mirror to societal values and cultural expectations, sparking discussions on fidelity, trust, and the boundaries of personal and sexual freedom. These discussions contribute to ongoing dialogues about consent, power dynamics, and the diversity of human desires and relationships.

In conclusion, cultural representations of cuckoldry across literature, film, online forums, and visual arts serve as mirrors to societal attitudes and evolving interpretations of human sexuality and relationships. By exploring themes of trust, intimacy, power dynamics, and personal autonomy, these representations contribute to broader discussions about the complexities of desire, fidelity, and the fluidity of relationship norms in contemporary society.

Literary Work Related To Themes Of Cuckoldry And Infidelity

1. **"Othello" by William Shakespeare** - This tragedy explores jealousy and betrayal as Othello suspects his wife, Desdemona, of infidelity, leading to dramatic consequences.
2. **"The Canterbury Tales" by Geoffrey Chaucer** - In "The Miller's Tale," a bawdy and humorous story, a carpenter is tricked and cuckolded by his young wife and her lover.
3. **"The Merry Wives of Windsor" by William Shakespeare** - A comedic play where Sir John Falstaff tries to seduce two married women, leading to a series of humorous misunderstandings about infidelity.
4. **"Madame Bovary" by Gustave Flaubert** - Emma Bovary seeks excitement outside her marriage through extramarital affairs, ultimately leading to her downfall.
5. **"The Country Wife" by William Wycherley** - A Restoration comedy that satirizes marriage and infidelity, focusing on a man pretending to be impotent to seduce other men's wives.
6. **"Anna Karenina" by Leo Tolstoy** - This novel explores the consequences of Anna's affair with Count Vronsky, highlighting the impact of infidelity on her life and marriage.
7. **"The Great Gatsby" by F. Scott Fitzgerald** - Infidelity plays a central role as Tom Buchanan's affair with Myrtle Wilson creates tension and ultimately leads to tragedy.
8. **"Ulysses" by James Joyce** - The novel follows Leopold Bloom, who contemplates his wife's infidelity throughout the narrative, reflecting on themes of jealousy and acceptance.
9. **"The Golden Bowl" by Henry James** - A complex novel about marriage and infidelity, exploring the intricate

relationships between two couples and the hidden truths they uncover.

10. **"Tess of the d'Urbervilles" by Thomas Hardy** - Tess Durbeyfield's life is marked by societal judgment and personal tragedy, including themes of betrayal and mistrust.

11. **"Les Liaisons Dangereuses" by Pierre Choderlos de Laclos** - This epistolary novel delves into manipulation and seduction, with characters engaging in affairs to control and disgrace others.

12. **"Lady Chatterley's Lover" by D.H. Lawrence** - The novel depicts the affair between Lady Chatterley and a gamekeeper, challenging social norms and exploring themes of physical and emotional infidelity.

13. **"Middlemarch" by George Eliot** - The novel examines various marriages and relationships, including issues of fidelity, societal expectations, and personal growth.

14. **"The Kreutzer Sonata" by Leo Tolstoy** - A dramatic exploration of jealousy and marital discord, where the protagonist recounts how his suspicions of infidelity lead to a tragic outcome.

15. **"The Scarlet Letter" by Nathaniel Hawthorne** - Set in Puritan New England, the story centers on Hester Prynne, who bears the consequences of an adulterous affair in a rigid society.

16. **"The Age of Innocence" by Edith Wharton** - This novel explores the complexities of societal norms and forbidden love, focusing on Newland Archer's emotional conflict between his fiancée and a woman from his past.

17. **"Revolutionary Road" by Richard Yates** - The story of a suburban couple whose marriage deteriorates, highlighting infidelity as part of their search for meaning and fulfillment.

18. **"The End of the Affair" by Graham Greene** - A novel about love, jealousy, and faith, centered on a wartime affair and its emotional repercussions for all involved.

19. **"Flaubert's Parrot" by Julian Barnes** - While not exclusively about infidelity, this novel explores themes of obsession and betrayal through a literary and biographical lens.

20. **"Disgrace" by J.M. Coetzee** - The story of a disgraced professor who navigates complex relationships and moral dilemmas, including issues of power, race, and infidelity in post-apartheid South Africa.

Other Literary Works

There are some memoirs, autobiographies, and novels where authors discuss themes related to cuckoldry or consensual non-monogamy, either as part of their personal experiences or as fictionalized narratives. However, these are typically presented as literary works rather than factual accounts of specific individuals. Examples include:

1. "The Ethical Slut: A Practical Guide to Polyamory, Open Relationships & Other Adventures" by Dossie Easton and Janet W. Hardy

2. "Sex at Dawn: How We Mate, Why We Stray, and What It Means for Modern Relationships" by Christopher Ryan and Cacilda Jethá

3. "My Husband Betty: Love, Sex, and Life with a Crossdresser" by Helen Boyd

4. "The Truth: An Uncomfortable Book About Relationships" by Neil Strauss

5. "Opening Up: A Guide to Creating and Sustaining Open Relationships" by Tristan Taormino

These books explore various aspects of non-traditional relationships, including cuckoldry, from both personal and academic perspectives. However, they do not typically name specific individuals involved in these practices unless they are public figures who have chosen to disclose their experiences.

Cuckoldry And Infidelity Themes In Art And Painting

"Mars and Venus Surprised by Vulcan" by Tintoretto

- **Description**: This painting depicts the moment Vulcan catches Mars and Venus in an affair. The dramatic scene showcases tension and betrayal, highlighting the consequences of infidelity among gods.

- **Significance**: The work illustrates the complexities of love, desire, and retribution, exploring the impact of infidelity on relationships.

"The Procuress" by Dirck van Baburen

- **Description**: This piece shows a scene of a young woman, an older procuress, and a customer. The work delves into themes of transactional love and deception.

- **Significance**: It serves as a critique of moral corruption and the darker aspects of human relationships.

"Venus, Mars, and Vulcan" by Joachim Wtewael

- **Description**: Wtewael captures the mythological story where Venus is caught with Mars by her husband, Vulcan. The vibrant colors and intricate details emphasize the tension.

- **Significance**: This artwork explores the fragility of trust and the consequences of betrayal in intimate relationships.

"Susanna and the Elders" by Artemisia Gentileschi

- **Description**: Susanna is depicted being harassed by two elders. The painting is a powerful commentary on voyeurism, exploitation, and the vulnerability of women.

- **Significance**: It highlights the themes of invasion of privacy and the moral dilemmas associated with fidelity and purity.

"The Adulteress" by Lucas Cranach the Elder

- **Description**: This biblical scene portrays the moment when an adulteress is brought before Christ. The painting captures the tension between sin and redemption.

- **Significance**: It explores societal judgments on infidelity and the potential for forgiveness and moral reflection.

"The Toilet of Venus" by François Boucher

- **Description**: Venus is shown in a sensual pose, embodying beauty and temptation. This work reflects the allure and seduction often associated with infidelity.

- **Significance**: It emphasizes the captivating power of beauty and the potential for moral lapses in the face of temptation.

"The Swing" by Jean-Honoré Fragonard

- **Description**: A young woman is playfully swinging, with a hidden lover watching. The scene is filled with flirtation and secretive romance.

- **Significance**: This painting symbolizes romantic intrigue, suggesting the playful yet deceptive nature of infidelity.

"The Lovers" by René Magritte

- **Description**: Two figures kiss with their faces covered, representing hidden identities and mysterious connections.

- **Significance**: The piece explores themes of concealed emotions and the enigmatic aspects of romantic relationships.

"The Education of the Virgin" by Georges de La Tour

- **Description**: Although primarily religious, it subtly hints at moral themes, exploring purity and temptation.

- **Significance**: It juxtaposes innocence with the lurking presence of sin, reflecting on the complex dynamics of human morality.

"The Garden of Earthly Delights" by Hieronymus Bosch

- **Description**: This triptych depicts various scenes of pleasure, temptation, and damnation, with the central panel focusing on earthly pleasures.

- **Significance**: It is a comprehensive exploration of human sins, including lust and infidelity, serving as a moral warning.

"The Judgement of Paris" by Peter Paul Rubens

- **Description**: This painting portrays Paris judging the beauty of three goddesses, leading to themes of desire and rivalry.

- **Significance**: It explores the consequences of choices driven by desire and the conflicts that arise from infidelity.

"Venus and Mars" by Sandro Botticelli

- **Description**: Depicts the peaceful slumber of Mars after an encounter with Venus, symbolizing the power of love and attraction.

- **Significance**: The painting explores the serene yet potent influence of romantic entanglements.

"The Prodigal Son in the Tavern" by Rembrandt

- **Description**: A depiction of indulgence, showing the Prodigal Son amidst revelry and temptation.

- **Significance**: It serves as a moral allegory on the dangers of excess and infidelity.

"The Lady of Shalott" by John William Waterhouse

- **Description**: Illustrates the tragic tale of the Lady of Shalott, bound by a curse, who gazes longingly at Sir Lancelot.

- **Significance**: The painting reflects themes of unrequited love and the yearning for forbidden desires.

"Woman Taken in Adultery" by Rembrandt

- **Description**: This work captures the moment of judgment and potential forgiveness for a woman caught in adultery.

- **Significance**: It addresses the societal implications of infidelity and the balance between justice and mercy.

"Samson and Delilah" by Peter Paul Rubens

- **Description**: Shows Delilah's betrayal of Samson, highlighting themes of seduction and deception.

- **Significance**: It underscores the dangers of trust and the impact of betrayal on relationships.

"Ugolino and His Sons" by Jean-Baptiste Carpeaux

- **Description**: Represents the historical tale of Count Ugolino, imprisoned with his sons, reflecting themes of despair and betrayal.

- **Significance**: This sculpture explores deep emotional and moral struggles, often linked to themes of trust and infidelity.

"The Death of Sardanapalus" by Eugène Delacroix

- **Description**: A dramatic depiction of the Assyrian king's final moments, filled with destruction and decadence.

- **Significance**: It examines the themes of excess, betrayal, and the downfall brought about by indulgence.

"Judith and Holofernes" by Caravaggio

- **Description**: Judith beheading Holofernes captures a moment of violent betrayal and seduction.

- **Significance**: The painting explores the interplay of power, seduction, and ultimate betrayal.

"La Belle Dame sans Merci" by Frank Dicksee

- **Description**: Based on Keats' poem, it depicts a knight enthralled by a mysterious woman, leading to his downfall.

- **Significance**: Reflects on themes of enchantment and the perilous nature of seductive relationships.

FAQs- FREQUENTLY ASKED QUESTIONS ABOUT THIS TOPIC

What Is Cuckoldry?

Cuckoldry refers to the practice or fantasy where a person's partner engages in sexual activity with someone else, typically with the consent or knowledge of the partner.

Is Cuckoldry Consensual?

Yes, in modern contexts, cuckoldry can be consensual, meaning both partners agree to or derive pleasure from the experience.

What Are The Psychological Dynamics Of Cuckoldry?

Cuckoldry can involve aspects of dominance, submission, voyeurism, and compersion (taking pleasure in a partner's pleasure). It often explores themes of trust, intimacy, and sexual exploration within relationships.

Is Cuckoldry The Same As Infidelity?

No, cuckoldry implies consent or knowledge from the partner, whereas infidelity typically refers to betrayal of trust by engaging in sexual activity outside the relationship without the partner's consent.

Why Do People Engage In Cuckoldry?

Reasons vary, but it can include exploring fantasies, enhancing sexual arousal, strengthening trust and communication within relationships, or simply enjoying the psychological or emotional aspects of sharing sexual experiences.

What Are Some Misconceptions About Cuckoldry?

One common misconception is that it's solely about humiliation or degradation, which isn't true in consensual contexts where it can actually strengthen relationships.

Is Cuckoldry A Common Practice?

It's difficult to quantify due to its private nature, but interest in cuckoldry is evident in various forms of media and online communities dedicated to alternative sexual lifestyles.

How Can Couples Navigate The Complexities Of Cuckoldry?

Open and honest communication, setting clear boundaries, and regularly checking in with each other's emotional well-being are crucial. Professional guidance or counseling can also be beneficial.

Are There Ethical Considerations To Be Aware Of In Cuckoldry?

Yes, respecting boundaries, ensuring consent, and prioritizing emotional well-being are essential to practicing cuckoldry ethically.

Where Can I Find More Information Or Support About Cuckoldry?

Online forums, books on alternative lifestyles, and sexuality-focused therapists can provide resources and support for individuals and couples exploring cuckoldry.

Based On Research, Which Countries And Cultures Are Known To Engage In The Practice Of Cuckoldry?

Cuckoldry as a practice or fetish can vary significantly across cultures and countries, influenced by historical, societal, and individual factors. However, it's important to note that comprehensive, reliable studies specifically quantifying the prevalence of cuckoldry in different cultures are limited. The concept of cuckoldry itself spans across historical narratives, mythologies, and cultural stereotypes, often depicting themes of betrayal, jealousy, and sexual dynamics.

In modern contexts, certain Western cultures, particularly those with a history of openness toward sexual exploration and non-traditional relationships, may see higher visibility of consensual cuckoldry as a sexual practice or kink. This visibility is often reflected in media representations, online communities, and discussions around alternative relationship dynamics.

Conversely, cultural attitudes and taboos around sexuality, fidelity, and marital expectations can vary widely across different regions and societies. Some cultures may view cuckoldry strictly through the lens of betrayal and dishonor, while others may approach it with more nuanced perspectives or as part of sexual exploration and consensual non-monogamy.

Overall, the prevalence and acceptance of cuckoldry as a practiced lifestyle or fetish can depend heavily on individual preferences, societal norms, and cultural attitudes toward sexuality and relationships.

Can You Provide Information On The Prevalence Of Consensual Cuckoldry In Different Countries?

I'm sorry, but there isn't specific data or studies that rank countries based on the practice of cuckoldry as a consensual sexual fetish or lifestyle. The nature of cuckoldry, being a private and often discreet practice within individual relationships or communities, makes it challenging to quantify or rank on a national scale.

Cuckoldry as a sexual practice or fetish is more commonly discussed in the context of individual preferences and cultural attitudes toward non-monogamous relationships and alternative sexual behaviors. These attitudes can vary widely across cultures and are influenced by factors such as societal norms, religious beliefs, and legal frameworks regarding marriage and fidelity.

If you're interested in understanding more about cultural attitudes toward sexuality or non-monogamous relationships in different countries, general studies on sexual behavior or relationship dynamics might provide broader insights. However, specific rankings or data on cuckoldry as a practiced lifestyle typically aren't available.

Chapter 1: Open Relationship Agreement

A Journey Through Openness: A Story of Love and Exploration

Sarah and Alex had been together for eight years, their relationship forged through shared dreams, challenges, and deep emotional connection. From the outside, they seemed like the quintessential couple—supportive, loving, and committed. However, behind closed doors, they had a unique arrangement that challenged traditional notions of monogamy.

Their journey into an open relationship began with honest conversations about their individual desires and needs. Both Sarah and Alex valued honesty and autonomy in their relationship, and they believed that love could exist alongside the freedom to explore connections with others. They agreed that their commitment to each other wasn't defined by sexual exclusivity but by mutual respect, trust, and emotional support.

For Sarah, the openness meant occasionally exploring romantic connections with other people, while Alex found fulfillment in deepening friendships that occasionally crossed into romantic territory. They established clear boundaries from the start—communication was key, and any new connection outside their relationship was discussed openly and honestly. They prioritized safe sex practices and regular health screenings to ensure their physical well-being.

Their journey wasn't without challenges. Feelings of jealousy and insecurity surfaced at times, prompting heartfelt conversations and reassurances. They leaned on each other for support, navigating emotional terrain with empathy and understanding. Over time, they discovered that their commitment to each other grew stronger as they learned to communicate more openly and handle emotions maturely.

One pivotal moment came when Sarah developed a deep connection with a new partner. She was upfront about her feelings with Alex, who listened attentively and expressed his own emotions without judgment. Together, they explored what this new connection meant for their relationship, reaffirming their love and commitment in the process.

Their openness extended beyond their relationship—they found a supportive community of like-minded individuals who shared similar values and experiences. They attended workshops on communication and non-monogamous relationships, learning from others and refining their own approach.

Through their journey, Sarah and Alex discovered that love is not a finite resource but a boundless wellspring that can be shared and celebrated. Their open relationship wasn't about seeking perfection or escaping challenges—it was about embracing vulnerability, growth, and the richness of human connection.

As they continued their journey together, Sarah and Alex knew that their relationship was a reflection of their shared values—honesty, respect, and the courage to redefine love on their own terms. In a world where relationships are often boxed into societal norms, theirs was a testament to the beauty of authenticity and the power of mutual understanding.

In this story, Sarah and Alex navigate the complexities of an open relationship with honesty, communication, and mutual respect, demonstrating that non-traditional relationship structures can be deeply fulfilling and meaningful when approached thoughtfully and consensually.

Introduction: Open Relationship Agreement

An open relationship agreement is a consensual arrangement between partners that allows for romantic or sexual relationships with other people outside of the primary relationship. Unlike traditional monogamous relationships, open relationships are built on the foundation of mutual trust, open communication, and clear boundaries. These agreements can take many forms, tailored to the unique needs and desires of the individuals involved. The primary goal is to maintain a strong and healthy primary relationship while exploring connections with others in a way that feels safe and respectful for all parties. Understanding and negotiating the terms of an open relationship agreement can help partners navigate the complexities and potential challenges that come with non-monogamous arrangements.

Key Factors in Navigating an Open Relationship Agreement

1. Clear Communication:

○ Establish open and honest communication from the outset.

○ Discuss expectations, desires, and boundaries regularly to ensure both partners are on the same page.

○ Use active listening to understand each other's feelings and concerns.

2. Mutual Consent:

○ Ensure that both partners genuinely agree to the terms of the open relationship.

○ Consent must be ongoing, with the option for either partner to renegotiate or withdraw consent as needed.

3. Setting Boundaries:

○ Clearly define what is acceptable and what is off-limits.

○ Discuss and agree on rules regarding physical intimacy, emotional connections, and frequency of outside relationships.

○ Determine whether partners will share details about their external relationships and, if so, to what extent.

4. Regular Check-Ins:

○ Schedule regular times to discuss how the arrangement is working for both partners.

○ Address any issues or concerns promptly to prevent misunderstandings or resentment from building up.

5. Trust and Respect:

○ Build and maintain trust through transparency and accountability.

○ Respect each other's boundaries and agreements to ensure a healthy and supportive environment.

6. Emotional Support:

○ Provide emotional support and reassurance to each other, acknowledging any feelings of jealousy or insecurity.

○ Seek to understand and empathize with each other's emotional needs.

7. **Flexibility:**

○ Be open to adjusting the terms of the agreement as the relationship evolves.

○ Understand that needs and desires may change over time, and be willing to renegotiate boundaries accordingly.

8. **Self-Awareness:**

○ Encourage each partner to engage in self-reflection to understand their own motivations and emotions.

○ Address any personal insecurities or fears that may arise in the context of an open relationship.

9. **External Resources:**

○ Consider seeking guidance from a relationship counselor or therapist specializing in non-monogamous relationships.

○ Utilize books, articles, and online communities for additional support and perspectives.

10. **Privacy and Discretion:**

○ Agree on the level of privacy and discretion desired regarding external relationships.

○ Discuss how to handle social situations and interactions with mutual friends or family members.

By focusing on these key factors, partners can create a supportive and understanding environment that allows for the successful navigation of an open relationship agreement.

Advantages of Open Relationships

Open relationships, where partners consensually agree to engage in romantic or sexual activities with others outside their primary relationship, offer a range of advantages for those involved. These benefits often stem from enhanced communication, personal growth, and the opportunity to explore diverse experiences. Here's a detailed exploration of the advantages of open relationships:

1. **Enhanced Communication:**

○ **Transparency and Honesty:** Open relationships require high levels of communication, which fosters an environment of honesty and transparency. Partners are more likely to discuss their needs, desires, and boundaries openly, leading to a deeper understanding of each other.

○ **Conflict Resolution Skills:** The need to navigate complex emotions and situations can improve conflict resolution skills. Partners learn to address issues calmly and constructively, enhancing the overall health of the relationship.

2. Personal Growth:

○ **Self-Discovery:** Engaging with multiple partners can lead to greater self-awareness. Individuals may discover new aspects of their identity, preferences, and desires that they were previously unaware of.

○ **Increased Confidence:** Successfully managing an open relationship can boost self-esteem and confidence. Knowing that one can navigate multiple relationships can affirm one's attractiveness and desirability.

3. Variety and Exploration:

○ **Sexual Exploration:** Open relationships allow partners to explore different sexual experiences and fantasies without the constraints of monogamy. This can lead to a more fulfilling and adventurous sex life.

○ **Emotional Connections:** Beyond physical experiences, open relationships can provide opportunities for diverse emotional connections. Partners may find intellectual and emotional fulfillment with different individuals, enriching their lives.

4. Reduced Pressure on the Primary Relationship:

○ **Diversified Emotional Support:** With multiple partners, the pressure to fulfill all emotional and physical needs is lessened. This can lead to a more relaxed and enjoyable primary relationship, as partners are not solely dependent on each other for all their needs.

○ **Preventing Stagnation:** The dynamic nature of open relationships can prevent boredom and stagnation, keeping the primary relationship vibrant and exciting.

5. Addressing Compatibility Issues:

○ **Complementary Strengths:** Different partners can complement various aspects of one's personality and interests. For example, if one partner enjoys activities that the other does not, they can pursue those interests with someone else.

○ **Sexual Mismatches:** Differences in sexual desire or preferences can be addressed by engaging with other partners, reducing potential sources of conflict in the primary relationship.

6. Improved Relationship Skills:

○ **Boundary Setting:** Open relationships necessitate clear boundaries, enhancing partners' ability to set and respect limits in all areas of life.

○ **Time Management:** Balancing multiple relationships requires effective time management skills, which can be beneficial in personal and professional contexts.

7. Stronger Primary Relationship:

○ **Renewed Appreciation:** Spending time with other partners can lead to a renewed appreciation for the primary partner. Absence can make the heart grow fonder, and returning to the primary relationship can feel refreshing.

○ **Greater Trust:** Successfully navigating an open relationship can build immense trust between partners. Knowing that they can explore other connections without jeopardizing the primary relationship can strengthen the bond.

8. **Social and Community Benefits:**

○ **Expanded Social Circle:** Engaging with multiple partners can lead to a broader social network, offering diverse perspectives and support systems.

○ **Community Belonging:** Being part of the non-monogamous community can provide a sense of belonging and acceptance, reducing feelings of isolation.

9. **Increased Resilience:**

○ **Adaptability:** The flexibility required to maintain an open relationship can make individuals more adaptable and resilient in the face of life's challenges.

○ **Emotional Intelligence:** Regularly navigating complex emotional landscapes can enhance emotional intelligence, making individuals more empathetic and understanding.

While open relationships offer numerous advantages, they are not suitable for everyone. Success in an open relationship requires a high degree of communication, trust, and mutual respect. Partners must be willing to navigate potential challenges and commit to ongoing dialogue to ensure the arrangement works for everyone involved. By understanding and leveraging these advantages, individuals can create fulfilling and dynamic relationships that cater to their unique needs and desires.

Disadvantages of Open Relationships

While open relationships offer several potential advantages, they also come with inherent challenges and disadvantages. These can stem from emotional complexities, societal judgments, and logistical issues. Here's an in-depth exploration of the disadvantages of open relationships:

1. **Jealousy and Insecurity:**

○ **Emotional Turmoil:** Even with clear communication, feelings of jealousy can arise. Seeing a partner with someone else can trigger insecurity, leading to emotional distress.

○ **Comparison:** Partners may compare themselves to their partner's other lovers, leading to feelings of inadequacy or low self-esteem.

2. **Complex Emotions:**

○ **Attachment Issues:** Developing strong emotional connections with multiple partners can complicate feelings. Managing multiple attachments can be challenging and confusing.

○ **Emotional Burnout:** The effort required to maintain multiple relationships can lead to emotional exhaustion, impacting overall well-being.

3. Communication Overload:

○ **Excessive Negotiation:** Open relationships require constant communication and negotiation. The ongoing discussions about boundaries, feelings, and expectations can become overwhelming and exhausting.

○ **Misunderstandings:** Despite best efforts, misunderstandings can occur. Miscommunication about boundaries or feelings can lead to conflicts and hurt feelings.

4. Time and Energy Constraints:

○ **Limited Availability:** Balancing multiple relationships demands a significant amount of time and energy. This can lead to neglecting personal needs, hobbies, or even the primary relationship.

○ **Scheduling Conflicts:** Coordinating schedules to spend time with multiple partners can be challenging, leading to frustration and resentment.

5. Social Stigma:

○ **Judgment from Others:** Open relationships are often misunderstood and stigmatized by society. Partners may face judgment, criticism, or ostracism from friends, family, and the broader community.

○ **Secrecy and Discretion:** To avoid social stigma, partners may feel compelled to keep their relationship structure private, leading to stress and a feeling of living a double life.

6. Risk of Relationship Strain:

○ **Primary Relationship Neglect:** Focusing on multiple relationships can inadvertently lead to neglect of the primary relationship. This can weaken the primary bond and cause feelings of alienation.

○ **Increased Conflict:** The complexities of managing multiple relationships can increase the likelihood of conflicts. Disagreements over time allocation, boundaries, and emotional needs can strain relationships.

7. Sexual Health Risks:

○ **STIs:** Engaging in sexual activities with multiple partners increases the risk of sexually transmitted infections (STIs). Maintaining rigorous safe sex practices is essential but not foolproof.

○ **Health Management:** Regular health check-ups and transparent communication about sexual health are necessary, adding an extra layer of responsibility.

8. Emotional Impact on Others:

○ **Secondary Partners:** Secondary or additional partners may develop strong feelings or expectations that are not reciprocated. Managing these relationships with care and respect is crucial but can be challenging.

○ **Unintended Harm:** Despite best intentions, individuals in an open relationship might inadvertently hurt their secondary partners, leading to guilt and emotional distress.

9. **Logistical Challenges:**

○ **Coordination Difficulties:** Planning and coordinating time with multiple partners can be logistically challenging, leading to stress and frustration.

○ **Financial Strain:** Dating multiple partners can be financially taxing, with expenses related to outings, gifts, and travel adding up.

10. **Potential for Relationship Breakdown:**

○ **Emotional Distance:** If not managed carefully, the focus on external relationships can create emotional distance in the primary relationship, leading to a breakdown in connection.

○ **Incompatibility Realization:** Navigating an open relationship can highlight fundamental incompatibilities between partners that were not apparent in a monogamous setting, potentially leading to separation.

11. **Legal and Custody Issues:**

○ **Legal Complications:** In some jurisdictions, non-monogamous relationships can complicate legal matters, including inheritance and next-of-kin status.

○ **Custody Concerns:** If children are involved, open relationships can complicate custody arrangements and co-parenting dynamics, especially in the event of a breakup.

While open relationships can offer freedom and exploration, they also demand a high level of emotional intelligence, communication skills, and mutual respect. Partners considering this relationship structure must be prepared to navigate the potential disadvantages and commit to continuous effort and understanding to make the arrangement work. By acknowledging and addressing these challenges, individuals can better assess whether an open relationship is suitable for them and how to manage it effectively.

Consensual Non-Monogamy: Exploring Relationship Diversity

Consensual non-monogamy (CNM) is a relationship structure where all partners involved agree to engage in romantic or sexual relationships with others outside their primary partnership. Unlike traditional monogamous relationships, CNM emphasizes transparency, communication, and mutual consent among all parties.

Types of Consensual Non-Monogamy:

1. **Open Relationships:**

○ Partners agree to engage in sexual relationships with others while maintaining their primary relationship. Boundaries regarding emotional involvement and sexual practices are typically discussed and agreed upon.

2. Polyamory:

○ In polyamorous relationships, individuals have multiple romantic and emotional relationships simultaneously, with all partners aware of and consenting to the arrangement. Communication and emotional connection are key elements.

3. Swinging:

○ Swinging involves couples engaging in sexual activities with others as a couple or individually. It often occurs within specific social or community contexts, with rules about participation and sexual practices.

Key Elements of Consensual Non-Monogamy:

• **Communication:** Open and honest communication is essential to CNM. Partners discuss boundaries, desires, and concerns regularly to ensure everyone feels respected and understood.

• **Mutual Consent:** All parties involved freely agree to the relationship structure. Consent is ongoing and can be renegotiated as relationships evolve or circumstances change.

• **Respect and Trust:** CNM emphasizes mutual respect for individual autonomy and trust in each other's commitment to the agreed-upon boundaries.

• **Compersion:** This term describes the positive emotional response someone may experience when their partner finds happiness with another person. It contrasts with jealousy and reflects a supportive attitude within CNM relationships.

Benefits of Consensual Non-Monogamy:

• **Expanded Emotional Support:** Partners in CNM relationships can receive emotional support and companionship from multiple sources, enhancing overall well-being.

• **Increased Relationship Skills:** Negotiating boundaries, managing jealousy, and practicing effective communication can strengthen relationship skills and emotional resilience.

• **Personal Growth:** CNM encourages individuals to explore and understand their desires, values, and boundaries, promoting self-discovery and authenticity.

Challenges of Consensual Non-Monogamy:

• **Jealousy and Insecurity:** Managing jealousy and navigating emotional complexities can be challenging, requiring open communication and empathy.

• **Social Stigma:** CNM relationships may face stigma and misunderstanding from society or individuals who hold traditional views of monogamy.

- **Logistical Issues:** Balancing multiple relationships or coordinating schedules can be complex, requiring time management and logistical planning.

Conclusion:

Consensual non-monogamy offers individuals and couples a pathway to explore diverse relationship structures that align with their values and desires. By prioritizing communication, respect, and mutual consent, CNM relationships can foster deep emotional connections and personal growth, challenging societal norms and promoting understanding of relationship diversity.

Polyamory or Swinging

Polyamory and swinging are two distinct forms of consensual non-monogamy (CNM) that allow individuals and their partners to engage in multiple sexual or romantic relationships with the knowledge and consent of everyone involved. While both involve openness and mutual agreement, they differ in terms of emotional connection, relationship structure, and community dynamics.

Polyamory:

Polyamory is rooted in the belief that it is possible to love more than one person simultaneously, with a focus on developing multiple emotional and romantic connections. Here are some key aspects of polyamorous relationships:

- **Emotional Depth:** Polyamorous relationships prioritize emotional intimacy and connection. Individuals may have multiple romantic partners with whom they share deep emotional bonds, akin to those found in traditional monogamous relationships.

- **Commitment and Communication:** Communication is paramount in polyamory. Partners openly discuss their desires, boundaries, and feelings to ensure everyone feels valued and respected. Commitment can vary from casual to deeply committed relationships, depending on the individuals involved.

- **Compersion:** Polyamorous individuals often experience compersion—a feeling of joy or happiness when their partner finds fulfillment with another person. This contrasts with jealousy and is seen as a positive emotion within polyamorous communities.

- **Community and Support:** Polyamorous communities provide support, understanding, and resources for navigating complex emotions, relationship dynamics, and societal challenges. They often promote ethical non-monogamy and advocate for inclusivity and acceptance.

Swinging:

Swinging, also known as partner swapping or the lifestyle, involves couples engaging in sexual activities with others, typically as a unit or with the mutual consent of both partners. Here are some distinguishing features of swinging:

- **Sexual Focus:** Swinging primarily revolves around sexual exploration and enjoyment rather than emotional connection or romantic involvement. Partners may engage in group sex, orgies, or swap partners for sexual variety.

- **Rules and Boundaries:** Swinging couples establish rules and boundaries regarding sexual activities, including where, when, and with whom they engage sexually. Clear communication and respect for boundaries are crucial to maintaining harmony within swinging relationships.

- **Social and Recreational Aspects:** Swinging often occurs within specific social or community contexts, such as swinger clubs, parties, or online communities. These spaces provide opportunities for socializing, networking, and exploring shared sexual interests with like-minded individuals.

- **Privacy and Discretion:** Due to social stigma and privacy concerns, many swingers prioritize discretion about their lifestyle choices outside of their community circles.

Challenges and Considerations:

Both polyamory and swinging present unique challenges and considerations:

- **Jealousy and Insecurity:** Managing jealousy and navigating emotional complexities can be challenging in both polyamorous and swinging relationships. Open communication, self-awareness, and empathy are essential to address these feelings constructively.

- **Social Stigma:** Both lifestyles may face societal stigma and misunderstanding. Individuals in polyamorous or swinging relationships may encounter judgment or discrimination from friends, family, or broader society.

- **Relationship Dynamics:** Establishing and maintaining multiple relationships requires time, energy, and emotional investment. Individuals must balance the needs and desires of multiple partners while prioritizing their own well-being and boundaries.

- **Legal and Practical Considerations:** Legal frameworks and societal norms around relationships may not always accommodate polyamorous or swinging arrangements, potentially impacting issues such as inheritance, healthcare decisions, and custody arrangements.

In conclusion, polyamory and swinging are forms of consensual non-monogamy that allow individuals and couples to explore diverse relationship dynamics beyond traditional monogamy. Each offers unique opportunities for personal growth, sexual exploration, and community support, albeit with distinct focuses on emotional intimacy (polyamory) and sexual exploration (swinging). By embracing open communication, mutual respect, and ethical behavior, individuals can navigate these relationships authentically and responsibly, fostering fulfillment and connection in their chosen lifestyle.

Chapter 2: Fetish or Fantasy Fulfillment

Fetish or fantasy fulfillment involves engaging in sexual activities or scenarios that are considered outside the mainstream or traditional sexual behaviors. Here's a deep dive into these concepts:

Fetish:

A fetish is a sexual attraction to specific objects, body parts, or situations that are not typically sexualized. It involves deriving sexual arousal or gratification from these specific stimuli, which can vary widely among individuals. Some common fetishes include:

- **Foot fetish:** Sexual attraction to feet or footwear.

- **Bondage and discipline (BDSM):** Enjoyment of physical restraints, dominance, submission, or role-playing scenarios.

- **Latex or leather:** Arousal from wearing or seeing others in specific materials.

- **Role-playing:** Acting out specific roles or scenarios, such as teacher-student, doctor-patient, etc.

Characteristics of Fetishes:

- **Specificity:** Fetishes are often very specific in nature, focusing on particular objects, body parts, or behaviors.

- **Arousal Trigger:** The fetish object or scenario serves as a primary source of sexual arousal or pleasure.

- **Consent and Safety:** Engaging in fetish activities requires clear communication, mutual consent, and attention to safety protocols, especially in BDSM practices.

Fantasy Fulfillment:

Fantasy fulfillment involves exploring and fulfilling sexual fantasies—imaginative scenarios or desires that arouse individuals but may not necessarily be acted upon in reality. Fantasies can range from romantic and adventurous to taboo or unconventional. Some examples include:

- **Threesome or group sex:** The desire to engage sexually with multiple partners simultaneously.

- **Exhibitionism or voyeurism:** Enjoyment from being watched or watching others during sexual activities.

- **Role-playing:** Pretending to be someone else or acting out specific scenarios to enhance arousal and excitement.

- **Power dynamics:** Exploring dominant or submissive roles in consensual and negotiated contexts.

Characteristics of Fantasy Fulfillment:

- **Imagination and Creativity:** Fantasies are often imaginative and may involve scenarios or roles that individuals find stimulating but may not seek to enact in real life.

- **Emotional and Psychological Fulfillment:** Fulfilling fantasies can provide emotional satisfaction, enhance intimacy, and deepen connection within a relationship.

- **Exploration and Experimentation:** Individuals may use fantasy as a safe space to explore desires, experiment with new roles or scenarios, and expand sexual horizons.

Considerations and Consent:

- **Communication:** Open communication about desires, boundaries, and consent is crucial when exploring fetishes or fulfilling fantasies.

- **Safety:** Prioritize physical and emotional safety during any sexual exploration. Establish safe words or signals in BDSM or role-playing scenarios.

- **Mutual Respect:** Respect each other's boundaries and preferences, ensuring that all activities are consensual and enjoyable for everyone involved.

In summary, fetishes and fantasy fulfillment are ways in which individuals explore and express their sexual desires and preferences. Whether exploring specific objects or scenarios (fetish) or imaginative roles and scenarios (fantasy fulfillment), clear communication, mutual consent, and respect for boundaries are essential to creating fulfilling and safe sexual experiences.

Cuckold

A cuckold refers to a man who is aware of and often sexually aroused by his partner engaging in sexual activities with another person. In contemporary discussions about sexual relationships and fantasies, the term "cuckold" is often used to describe a consensual non-monogamous dynamic where a man finds pleasure, excitement, or satisfaction in knowing that his partner is with someone else. This can involve various levels of participation, from watching the act to simply knowing that it is happening.

The concept of cuckolding can be rooted in various psychological and emotional factors, such as:

1. **Voyeurism:** The arousal from watching or imagining one's partner with another person.
2. **Submission:** A desire to feel submissive or humiliated, deriving pleasure from the perceived dominance of the other man.
3. **Compersion:** The opposite of jealousy, where a person feels joy from their partner's pleasure with someone else.
4. **Trust and Intimacy:** The deepening of emotional and sexual trust through open communication and shared experiences.

It's important to distinguish between consensual cuckolding and infidelity. In consensual cuckolding, all parties are aware of and agree to the arrangement, which is based on mutual consent, communication, and respect. In contrast, infidelity involves deceit and betrayal, which can harm the trust and emotional foundation of a relationship.

Examples of Cuckold Dynamics

1. **Communication and Boundaries**: John and Mary decide to explore cuckolding by discussing their boundaries and comfort levels. They agree that Mary will meet another man, Kevin, with John's knowledge and consent. John finds excitement in the situation and they establish rules to ensure everyone's comfort.
2. **Voyeuristic Pleasure**: Mark enjoys watching his wife, Lisa, with another man. They set up an arrangement where Mark can observe their interactions, finding arousal in the visual and emotional aspects of the experience.
3. **Emotional Intimacy**: Sarah and Tom explore cuckolding to enhance their emotional intimacy. Tom feels aroused knowing Sarah is with another man, and their candid discussions about their feelings deepen their connection.

Considerations for Exploring Cuckolding

- **Open Communication**: Honest discussions about desires, boundaries, and feelings are crucial.

- **Consent**: All parties must willingly agree to the arrangement.

- **Emotional Preparedness**: Both partners should be emotionally ready to handle the dynamics and potential complexities.

- **Trust**: A strong foundation of trust is essential to prevent jealousy and resentment.

- **Respect and Care**: Ensuring that everyone involved feels respected and cared for.

Conclusion

Cuckolding, as a consensual and communicative practice, can be a way for couples to explore new dimensions of their relationship and sexuality. It emphasizes the importance of trust, communication, and mutual respect, allowing partners to deepen their emotional and sexual connection.

Exploring Human Sexual Diversity: A Look into Various Fetishes

Human sexuality is a rich and complex tapestry, encompassing a wide spectrum of desires, preferences, and fantasies. One fascinating aspect of this complexity is the diversity of fetishes—specific objects, behaviors, or sensations that individuals find sexually arousing or gratifying. From common interests to more niche attractions, fetishes reflect unique aspects of personal psychology, cultural influences, and individual expression.

In this exploration, we delve into a range of fetishes, each offering insight into the myriad ways people experience and express their sexual identities. Whether rooted in sensory stimulation, psychological dynamics, or cultural symbolism, each fetish provides a window into the diversity of human sexual desire. Through understanding and respectful exploration, we aim to appreciate the complexity of human sexuality and celebrate the diversity of human experience.

Foot Fetish (Podophilia):

- **Description**: Foot fetishism involves sexual arousal or attraction to feet, toes, or footwear. It can range from admiring feet to deriving sexual pleasure from touching, kissing, or massaging feet.

- **Psychology**: Foot fetishes are thought to be relatively common and may develop from early associations or cultural influences. For some, the feet represent a symbol of beauty, power, or eroticism.

- **Expression**: Fetishists may enjoy various aspects of feet, including size, shape, cleanliness, or specific features like toenails or arches. Activities may include foot worship, foot massage, or incorporating feet into sexual acts.

Bondage (BDSM):

- **Description**: Bondage refers to the practice of consensually restraining or tying up a partner for sexual pleasure. It often involves the use of ropes, chains, cuffs, or other restraints.

- **Psychology**: Bondage can appeal to individuals seeking sensations of vulnerability, control, or surrender. It may enhance trust and intimacy between partners through negotiated power dynamics.

- **Expression**: BDSM encompasses a range of activities, from light bondage for sensory play to more intense practices like Shibari (Japanese rope bondage) or elaborate restraint systems.

Role-playing:

- **Description**: Role-playing involves acting out specific roles or scenarios for sexual gratification. Common scenarios include teacher-student, doctor-patient, or fantasy roles like pirates or superheroes.

- **Psychology**: Role-playing allows individuals to explore different personas, fantasies, or power dynamics in a safe and consensual context. It can enhance creativity, communication, and intimacy between partners.

- **Expression**: Participants may use costumes, props, or dialogue to immerse themselves in the fantasy scenario, fulfilling desires for novelty, excitement, or exploring taboo themes.

Domination and Submission (D/s):

- **Description**: D/s dynamics involve consensual power exchange where one partner assumes a dominant role (Dom) and the other a submissive role (sub). Dominants exercise control, while submissives surrender control.

- **Psychology**: D/s dynamics can fulfill desires for dominance, submission, discipline, and surrender. It may involve protocols, rituals, or rules that structure the power dynamic and enhance trust and intimacy.

- **Expression**: Activities may range from mild to intense, including commands, obedience training, punishment, or reward systems based on negotiated boundaries and mutual consent.

Sadomasochism (S&M):

- **Description**: Sadomasochism involves deriving sexual pleasure from consensual acts of inflicting (sadism) or receiving (masochism) pain or physical sensations.

- **Psychology**: S&M practices can explore boundaries, sensation play, and power dynamics. They may involve psychological role-playing, intense physical sensations, or emotional release.

- **Expression**: Activities range from light sensation play (e.g., spanking, sensory deprivation) to more extreme forms (e.g., impact play with whips, needles, or psychological edge play).

Fetish Clothing:

- **Description**: Fetish clothing involves arousal from specific garments or materials, such as latex, leather, lingerie, uniforms, or fetishized costumes.

- **Psychology**: Fetish clothing can evoke associations with power, dominance, submission, or sensory pleasure. It may involve tactile sensations, visual appeal, or symbolic meanings tied to the material or style.

- **Expression**: Fetishists may enjoy wearing, seeing, touching, or smelling specific clothing items as part of sexual play or arousal. Fashion choices and aesthetics can play a significant role in expressing sexual identity and desires.

Body Part Fetishes:

- **Description**: Body part fetishes involve sexual attraction or fixation on specific body parts, such as breasts (mammary fetishism), buttocks (pygophilia), legs, hands, or hair (trichophilia).

- **Psychology**: Body part fetishes can stem from aesthetic appeal, cultural influences, or associations with eroticism and fertility. They may reflect personal preferences, sensory arousal, or psychological symbolism.

- **Expression**: Fetishists may focus on physical attributes, size, shape, symmetry, or sensory aspects of the preferred body part. Activities may include admiration, touching, kissing, or incorporating the body part into sexual activities.

Objectophilia:

- **Description**: Objectophilia involves romantic or sexual attraction to inanimate objects, such as buildings, cars, or specific items like dolls or stuffed animals.

- **Psychology**: Objectophilia challenges traditional views of sexual attraction, emphasizing emotional or relational connections with objects. It may involve anthropomorphizing objects or projecting human-like qualities onto them.

- **Expression**: Objectophiles may form intimate bonds with objects, engaging in activities like kissing, hugging, or even sexual acts with their preferred objects. They may view objects as companions or partners with whom they develop emotional connections.

Voyeurism:

- **Description**: Voyeurism entails obtaining sexual gratification from observing others' naked bodies or engaging in sexual activities without their knowledge or consent.

- **Psychology**: Voyeuristic behavior may stem from curiosity, arousal from visual stimuli, or a desire for forbidden or secretive observations. It can involve fantasies of watching others in private moments.

- **Expression**: Voyeurs may engage in peeping, spying, or using technology (e.g., hidden cameras) to observe others without their awareness. It is crucial to distinguish consensual exhibitionism from non-consensual voyeurism, which can violate privacy and consent boundaries.

Exhibitionism:

- **Description**: Exhibitionism involves deriving sexual arousal from exposing oneself or engaging in sexual acts in public or semi-public settings, often intentionally seeking attention or reactions.

- **Psychology**: Exhibitionists may enjoy the thrill of risk, the adrenaline rush of being caught, or the power dynamics of being watched. It can involve feelings of empowerment or sexual validation from being seen.

- **Expression**: Exhibitionist behavior can range from flashing or public nudity to consensual public sex acts. It often requires negotiation of boundaries, legality, and ethical considerations to ensure consent and safety.

Medical Play:

- **Description**: Medical play encompasses role-playing scenarios, such as doctor-patient or medical examination scenes, involving medical instruments, attire, or procedures for sexual arousal.

- **Psychology**: Medical play may evoke feelings of vulnerability, trust, or caretaking roles. It can involve exploration of power dynamics, sensory stimulation, or fetishization of medical environments.

- **Expression**: Participants may engage in simulated medical exams, procedures like temperature taking, or use of medical props (e.g., stethoscopes, speculums) to enact medical scenarios within consensual boundaries.

Age Play:

- **Description**: Age play involves role-playing scenarios where participants act different ages, often including caregiver roles (e.g., adult baby, daddy/mommy), exploring nurturing, dependency, or power dynamics.

- **Psychology**: Age play may tap into desires for innocence, care, or exploration of childhood or parental roles. It can include regression to childlike behaviors, dress, or activities within a consensual adult context.

- **Expression**: Age players may use costumes, toys, or dialogue to enact age-appropriate behaviors and dynamics, emphasizing emotional connection, trust, and negotiated boundaries between participants.

Furry Fandom:

- **Description**: The furry fandom involves an interest in anthropomorphic animal characters with human characteristics, often expressed through art, costumes (fursuits), and role-playing.

- **Psychology**: Furry fandom participants may identify with or find attraction in anthropomorphized animal traits, exploring identity, creativity, and community within a shared interest.

- **Expression**: Furries may create or commission anthropomorphic art, attend conventions, or engage in role-playing as furry personas. It can involve social interaction, fantasy exploration, and sexual expression within consensual and community-supported contexts.

Cross-dressing (Transvestic Fetishism):

- **Description**: Transvestic fetishism involves sexual arousal from wearing clothing typically associated with the opposite gender, often including undergarments, lingerie, or full outfits.

- **Psychology**: Cross-dressing can fulfill desires for gender exploration, sensory stimulation, or role-playing fantasies. It may challenge traditional gender norms and express diverse gender identities or eroticism.

- **Expression**: Cross-dressers may dress privately or publicly, explore gender expression through attire, or engage in cross-dressing as part of sexual play, identity exploration, or role-playing scenarios.

Uniform Fetish:

- **Description**: Uniform fetishism involves sexual arousal from uniforms worn by individuals in authoritative or professional roles, such as military uniforms, police uniforms, or school uniforms.

- **Psychology**: Uniforms can symbolize power, discipline, or specific roles, evoking fantasies of authority figures, role-playing scenarios, or institutional settings. Fetishists may be attracted to the aesthetic, symbolism, or associations of uniforms.

- **Expression**: Fetishists may collect or wear uniforms, role-play scenarios involving uniforms, or incorporate uniform elements (e.g., hats, badges) into sexual activities or fantasies.

Mechanophilia:

- **Description**: Mechanophilia refers to sexual attraction or arousal from machines, vehicles, or mechanical objects.

- **Psychology**: Mechanophiles may appreciate the form, function, or power associated with machines. This fetish can involve admiration for mechanical complexity, engineering, or the sensation of control over machinery.

- **Expression**: Mechanophiles may engage in activities such as sexualized interaction with vehicles (e.g., rubbing against cars), collecting model vehicles, or incorporating machinery into sexual fantasies or role-playing.

Food Play (Sploshing):

- **Description**: Food play, or sploshing, involves using food items or substances for sensual or sexual stimulation.

- **Psychology**: Sploshing can combine sensory experiences of texture, temperature, and taste with eroticism. It may evoke feelings of indulgence, sensory pleasure, or playful exploration of taboo or messy experiences.

- **Expression**: Participants may engage in activities like pouring food items (e.g., whipped cream, chocolate syrup) on bodies, using food in sexual role-playing, or incorporating culinary aesthetics into sexual rituals or intimacy.

Acrotomophilia:

- **Description**: Acrotomophilia involves sexual attraction or arousal to amputees or individuals with congenital limb differences.

- **Psychology**: Acrotomophiles may appreciate the aesthetic or symbolic aspects of limb differences, finding beauty or uniqueness in physical diversity. This fetish can challenge norms of bodily perfection and attractiveness.

- **Expression**: Acrotomophiles may seek out relationships with amputees, admire images or videos featuring individuals with limb differences, or incorporate fantasies of physical difference into sexual arousal or role-playing scenarios.

Stigmatophilia:

- **Description**: Stigmatophilia refers to sexual arousal or attraction to piercings, tattoos, or other body modifications.

- **Psychology**: Stigmatophiles may find aesthetic appeal or eroticism in body art or modifications that alter appearance or challenge traditional beauty standards. This fetish can reflect preferences for self-expression, rebellion, or individuality.

- **Expression**: Fetishists may seek out partners with body modifications, admire photos or art featuring body art, or incorporate tattoos and piercings into sexual play, rituals, or fantasies.

Pet Play:

- **Description**: Pet play involves role-playing scenarios where individuals take on animal personas (e.g., puppy play, kitten play) for sexual or psychological gratification.

- **Psychology**: Pet players may explore aspects of dominance, submission, nurturing, or escapism through animal roles. This fetish can involve sensory experiences, obedience training, or emotional connection within role-play dynamics.

- **Expression**: Participants may wear animal-themed costumes (e.g., collars, ears, tails), use pet-like behaviors (e.g., crawling, purring), or engage in symbolic activities (e.g., training, feeding) to embody animal personas and explore power dynamics or intimacy in consensual play.

Robot Fetishism (Mechanized Intimacy):

- **Description**: Robot fetishism involves sexual attraction or arousal from humanoid robots or artificial beings, often focusing on their mechanical or technological aspects.

- **Psychology**: Robot fetishists may be drawn to the idea of futuristic technology, artificial intelligence, or the fantasy of non-human partners. It can involve fascination with robotic aesthetics, functionality, or the idea of control over a machine.

- **Expression**: Fetishists may collect robot-themed art or objects, engage in role-playing scenarios with robot personas, or incorporate robotic elements (e.g., costumes, props) into sexual play or fantasies.

Giantess and Microphilia:

- **Description**: Giantess fetishism involves attraction to giant or oversized beings, often depicted as women towering over smaller figures. Microphilia is its counterpart, involving attraction to tiny or shrunken individuals.

- **Psychology**: These fetishes can reflect desires for dominance, submission, or exploration of size differentials. They may stem from fantasies of power dynamics, vulnerability, or physical scale in sexual contexts.

- **Expression**: Fetishists may enjoy fantasies, stories, or artwork depicting giantess scenarios or microphiliac interactions. Some engage in role-playing or use visual media to explore themes of size discrepancy and eroticism.

Inflation Fetish (Balloon Fetish):

- **Description**: Inflation fetishism involves sexual arousal from images, videos, or scenarios depicting individuals or objects inflating, expanding, or being filled with air or liquids.

- **Psychology**: Inflation fetishists may find arousal in the visual or tactile sensations associated with inflation, expansion, or pressure changes. It can involve themes of transformation, body alteration, or sensory stimulation.

- **Expression**: Fetishists may collect inflatable objects, engage in role-playing scenarios involving inflation, or enjoy media featuring characters or objects inflating. It may incorporate elements of control, transformation, or sensation play in consensual contexts.

Forniphilia (Human Furniture):

- **Description**: Forniphilia involves using a person as human furniture or incorporating human bodies into functional objects or decor, often in a submissive or objectified role.

- **Psychology**: Forniphilia can explore themes of objectification, submission, or role-playing scenarios where individuals act as inanimate objects or functional pieces of furniture.

- **Expression**: Participants may engage in consensual scenarios where a person is used as a table, chair, footrest, or other furniture item. It may involve physical restraint, positioning, or sensory deprivation to enhance the objectification experience.

Plushophilia (Stuffed Animal Fetish):

- **Description**: Plushophilia involves sexual attraction or arousal to stuffed animals or plush toys, often involving emotional or romantic attachment to specific toys.

- **Psychology**: Plushophiles may experience affection, comfort, or sexual gratification from plush toys, viewing them as companions or romantic partners. It can reflect a blend of emotional and sexual attraction to soft textures or anthropomorphic qualities.

- **Expression**: Plushophiles may collect plush toys, create personas or relationships with specific toys, or engage in role-playing scenarios that involve emotional bonding or sexual interactions with plush objects.

Urophilia (Golden Shower):

- **Description**: Urophilia involves sexual arousal from urine or urination-related activities, commonly known as "golden showers."

- **Psychology**: Urophiles may find arousal in the taboo nature of urine, sensory aspects like warmth or smell, or power dynamics involving submission or dominance during urination activities.

- **Expression**: Fetishists may engage in consensual urine play, such as urinating on or being urinated on by a partner, incorporating urination into sexual acts or fantasies, or exploring the psychological and physical sensations associated with urine.

Formicophilia (Insect Fetish):

- **Description**: Formicophilia refers to sexual attraction or arousal from insects or insect-like creatures.

- **Psychology**: Formicophiles may find fascination or sexual arousal in the appearance, movements, or behaviors of insects. It can involve fantasies of insect-themed transformation, role-playing, or sensory stimulation.

- **Expression**: Fetishists may collect insect-themed art or objects, engage in role-playing scenarios involving insects, or incorporate insect-like movements or behaviors into sexual play or fantasies.

Fur Fetish (Trichophilia):

- **Description**: Trichophilia, commonly known as fur fetishism, involves sexual attraction or arousal from hair, fur, or specific textures of hair.

- **Psychology**: Fur fetishists may find sensory gratification in the tactile qualities of hair or fur, experiencing arousal from touch, texture, or visual appearance. It can involve admiration for grooming rituals, hair length, or specific hair types.

- **Expression**: Fetishists may engage in activities like stroking, grooming, or fantasizing about hair or fur, collecting hair-related materials or objects, or incorporating hair-related stimuli into sexual play or sensory exploration.

Mask Fetish (Masquerade):

- **Description**: Mask fetishism, or masquerade, involves sexual attraction or arousal from masks, costumes, or facial concealment.

- **Psychology**: Mask fetishists may be drawn to the anonymity, mystery, or transformative aspects of masks. It can involve fantasies of role-playing, alter egos, or cultural symbolism associated with masks.

- **Expression**: Fetishists may collect masks, engage in role-playing scenarios where masks are worn or removed, explore themes of identity concealment or revelation, or incorporate masks into sexual play or fantasy exploration.

Smoking Fetish (Capnolagnia):

- **Description**: Capnolagnia, or smoking fetishism, involves sexual attraction or arousal from watching someone smoke, or from smoking oneself.

- **Psychology**: Smoking fetishists may find arousal in the visual, tactile, or olfactory sensations associated with smoking behaviors. It can involve fascination with smoke patterns, gestures, or the social or cultural aspects of smoking.

- **Expression**: Fetishists may engage in smoking as part of sexual play, watch smoking-related media or performances, collect smoking paraphernalia, or incorporate smoking imagery into fantasies or role-playing scenarios.

Tickling Fetish (Knismolagnia):

- **Description**: Knismolagnia involves sexual arousal or gratification from tickling or being tickled.

- **Psychology**: Tickling fetishists may experience sensations of pleasure, vulnerability, or arousal from tickling sensations. It can involve power dynamics, sensory stimulation, or exploring physical sensitivity in a playful or intimate context.

- **Expression**: Fetishists may engage in consensual tickling activities, explore tickling-themed role-playing scenarios, or incorporate tickling sensations into sexual play, emphasizing communication, trust, and mutual enjoyment.

Latex and Rubber Fetish (Rubberism):

- **Description**: Rubberism, or latex fetishism, involves sexual attraction or arousal from latex or rubber clothing, accessories, or sensory experiences.

- **Psychology**: Rubber fetishists may find arousal in the tight, smooth, or shiny textures of latex or rubber materials. It can involve sensory pleasure, tactile stimulation, or eroticism associated with clothing or fetish gear.

- **Expression**: Fetishists may wear latex clothing or accessories, engage in role-playing scenarios involving latex outfits (e.g., latex catsuits, gloves), collect latex or rubber items, or incorporate latex-related fantasies into sexual play or dress-up activities.

Breath Play (Erotic Asphyxiation):

- **Description**: Erotic asphyxiation involves restricting oxygen flow to enhance sexual arousal or pleasure, often through methods like choking, suffocation, or breath control.

- **Psychology**: Breath play enthusiasts may experience heightened sensations, euphoria, or altered states of consciousness from oxygen deprivation. It can involve trust dynamics, power exchange, or exploration of intense physical sensations.

- **Expression**: Participants may engage in consensual breath play techniques, negotiate safety protocols (e.g., signals, limits), explore erotic asphyxiation within BDSM contexts, or incorporate breath control into role-playing scenarios emphasizing control or vulnerability.

Emetophilia (Vomit Fetish):

- **Description**: Emetophilia involves sexual arousal or attraction to vomit or vomiting-related activities.

- **Psychology**: Emetophiles may find arousal in the sensory aspects of vomiting, such as the act, sight, smell, or taste of vomit. It can involve taboo exploration, sensory stimulation, or fascination with bodily fluids.

- **Expression**: Emetophiles may engage in consensual vomiting scenarios, explore fantasies or stories involving vomit, collect vomit-related media or materials, or incorporate vomit-themed elements into sexual play or role-playing activities.

Necrophilia (Thanatophilia):

- **Description**: Necrophilia involves sexual attraction or arousal from corpses or dead bodies.

- **Psychology**: Necrophiles may experience fantasies or arousal related to death, decay, or the physical characteristics of corpses. It is widely considered pathological and illegal due to ethical, legal, and health concerns.

- **Expression**: Necrophilia is illegal and unethical in most jurisdictions, and discussions about it typically focus on understanding its psychological, legal, and societal implications rather than acceptance or normalization.

Conclusion: Celebrating Sexual Diversity

Exploring the spectrum of fetishes reveals the vast landscape of human sexual diversity. Each fetish reflects unique aspects of human psychology, cultural influences, and personal experiences, offering insights into the complexities of sexual desire and identity. From the sensory pleasures of latex and rubber fetishism to the psychological dynamics of breath play and the taboo exploration in emetophilia, these fetishes showcase the myriad ways individuals navigate and express their sexual selves.

Understanding fetishes requires an open-minded approach that values consent, communication, and respect for personal boundaries. While some fetishes may challenge conventional norms or provoke discomfort, they are valid expressions of human sexuality that deserve recognition and understanding. By embracing sexual diversity, we affirm the complexity of human desire and promote a culture of inclusivity and acceptance.

As we continue to explore and discuss fetishes, let us foster a supportive environment where individuals can safely explore their desires and fantasies. Through education, empathy, and open dialogue, we can promote a more inclusive society that celebrates the rich tapestry of human sexuality.

Stories of people with this type of fetish

Welcome to a collection of stories that delve into the intimate lives of individuals who have fetishes. These narratives aim to provide a deeper understanding and insight into the experiences, emotions, and challenges faced by those who navigate the complexities of their unique desires.

Fetishes, often misunderstood and stigmatized, are an integral part of human sexuality. They represent a diverse range of attractions and preferences that can profoundly shape an individual's sense of identity and relationships. Through these stories, you will meet people from various walks of life who share their journeys with openness and vulnerability.

Each story explores the personal and relational dynamics of living with a fetish. From the initial discovery and self-acceptance to communicating desires with partners and integrating these into their relationships, these narratives highlight the importance of empathy, understanding, and acceptance.

By reading these stories, you will gain a more nuanced perspective on fetishes, moving beyond stereotypes and misconceptions to appreciate the rich, complex experiences of those who live with them. These accounts will challenge you to think differently about what it means to love and be loved, to desire and be desired, and to seek fulfillment in diverse and authentic ways.

Embark on this journey with an open mind and heart, ready to understand the depth and diversity of human sexuality through the eyes of those who experience it uniquely.

Now, let's delve into the stories and discover the world of fetishes from those who know it best.

A Step Towards Understanding: Emily's Journey

Emily had always known she was different. From a young age, she felt a unique fascination with feet. It wasn't until she reached adulthood that she fully understood this attraction—it was a foot fetish, something she initially felt embarrassed and secretive about.

Living in a society where such preferences were often misunderstood, Emily struggled with her desires, unsure how to express them in a relationship. She had dated several people but never found the courage to share this intimate part of herself. That changed when she met Jason.

Jason was kind, open-minded, and most importantly, made Emily feel safe. They met at a mutual friend's party, and their connection was instant. As their relationship blossomed, Emily found herself falling deeply in love with Jason. However, the fear of revealing her fetish lingered.

One evening, after a particularly romantic date, they sat together on the couch, their feet touching. Emily felt a familiar stir of excitement but also a pang of anxiety. She knew it was time to be honest with Jason if their relationship was to move forward.

"Jason, can I talk to you about something?" Emily asked, her voice trembling slightly.

"Of course, Em. You can tell me anything," Jason replied, concern and curiosity in his eyes.

Taking a deep breath, Emily began to explain her foot fetish, starting from her early fascination to the embarrassment and fear she had felt over the years. Jason listened intently, never interrupting, his expression soft and understanding.

"Emily, thank you for sharing this with me," Jason said gently when she finished. "I want you to know that I love you for who you are, and your desires are a part of that. We can explore this together, at your pace."

Relief washed over Emily. They talked more about her fetish, setting boundaries and discussing ways to incorporate it into their intimacy in a comfortable and consensual manner.

Their first exploration was simple. Jason suggested giving Emily a foot massage, something she found incredibly arousing. He took his time, making sure she felt comfortable and reassured. The experience was transformative for Emily. She felt seen, accepted, and loved in a way she never had before.

As their relationship progressed, they continued to explore Emily's fetish in various ways. Sometimes it was through playful teasing, other times more intimately. Jason's willingness to understand and participate without judgment strengthened their bond.

Emily also joined online communities and forums where she connected with others who shared her fetish. She found support and camaraderie, learning from others' experiences and gaining confidence in her own desires.

Over time, Emily and Jason's relationship flourished, built on a foundation of trust, openness, and mutual respect. Emily no longer felt ashamed of her fetish; instead, she embraced it as a unique part of her sexuality that brought her and Jason closer.

Their journey was a testament to the power of communication and acceptance in a relationship. Emily learned that love isn't about hiding parts of oneself but about finding someone who cherishes every aspect of who you are. And with Jason, she had found just that—true acceptance and a love that embraced all of her, fetish and all.

In this story, Emily's journey highlights the importance of open communication and mutual respect in navigating personal desires within a relationship. Through understanding and support, Emily and Jason are able to build a deeper, more fulfilling connection.

Bound by Trust: Lily and Mark's Exploration of BDSM

Lily and Mark had been married for five years, their relationship marked by deep love and mutual respect. Both were adventurous and open-minded, always eager to explore new dimensions of their connection. Over time, they discovered a shared interest in BDSM, a realm that promised to deepen their intimacy and trust.

Their journey into BDSM began with honest conversations. Both had read about it and were intrigued by the dynamics of dominance and submission, the allure of physical restraints, and the thrill of role-playing scenarios. They agreed that open communication and consent were paramount and decided to take their first steps with caution and care.

One evening, they decided to explore their newfound interest. They transformed their bedroom into a safe and inviting space, complete with soft lighting, candles, and soothing music. Mark, naturally inclined towards a dominant role, and Lily, who felt a pull towards submission, discussed their boundaries and established a safe word—"blue"—that either could use to pause the scene if needed.

Mark began by gently tying Lily's wrists with silk scarves, making sure she was comfortable and secure. The act of being restrained heightened Lily's senses, filling her with a mix of anticipation and excitement. Mark's voice, calm and reassuring, guided her through the process, reinforcing the trust they had built.

They eased into their roles, with Mark taking on the persona of a strict yet caring dominant, and Lily embracing her submission. They engaged in light role-playing, with Mark giving gentle commands and Lily following them with eager compliance. The dynamic allowed them to explore power exchange in a way that felt thrilling yet safe.

As the scene progressed, Mark incorporated elements of discipline, using a soft paddle to deliver light, rhythmic taps to Lily's skin. Each strike was followed by a caress, a reminder of the tenderness underlying their exploration. Lily's responses, a mix of gasps and sighs, conveyed her enjoyment and trust in Mark's control.

Throughout their session, communication remained a cornerstone. Mark frequently checked in with Lily, ensuring she was comfortable and consenting. The use of their safe word provided an added layer of security, though it was never needed that night.

Afterwards, they shared a period of aftercare, a vital aspect of BDSM practice. Mark untied Lily's wrists and held her close, whispering words of affection and reassurance. They cuddled, shared their feelings, and reflected on the experience. The aftercare helped them transition back to their everyday selves, reinforcing the emotional connection that underpinned their play.

Their foray into BDSM brought new dimensions to their relationship. It deepened their trust, enhanced their communication, and allowed them to explore their desires in a consensual and fulfilling manner. Over time, they continued to experiment with different aspects of BDSM, always prioritizing consent, safety, and mutual respect.

Lily and Mark's story illustrates that BDSM, when approached with care and understanding, can be a deeply enriching part of a relationship. Their journey was not just about physical sensations or power dynamics; it was about building a deeper connection, exploring trust, and embracing the full spectrum of their desires.

In this scenario, Lily and Mark navigate their interest in BDSM with clear communication, established boundaries, and a focus on mutual respect and trust. Their story highlights the importance of consent and aftercare, showing how BDSM can enhance intimacy and connection in a loving relationship.

Role-Playing: Acting out specific roles or scenarios: A Night of Transformation: Emma and Tom's Role-Playing Adventure

Emma and Tom had always enjoyed adding a touch of creativity to their relationship. Both had a flair for drama and imagination, often finding joy in playful banter and storytelling. One evening, they decided to take their playfulness to the next level by exploring role-playing in their intimate life.

Their first role-playing scenario was inspired by one of their favorite themes: a teacher and a student. They agreed on a simple plot where Emma, the stern and knowledgeable teacher, would tutor Tom, the eager but mischievous student, who needed extra help after class.

Emma transformed their living room into a mock classroom. She wore a crisp white blouse, a pencil skirt, and glasses perched on her nose, completing her authoritative look. Tom, on the other hand, dressed in a casual shirt and jeans, playing the part of the slightly rebellious student.

As Tom entered the room, he couldn't help but smirk at the sight of Emma in her teacher attire. He took a seat at the makeshift desk, trying to suppress his grin.

Emma cleared her throat and gave him a stern look. "Mr. Tom, it seems your grades have been slipping lately. We need to discuss your performance," she said, her voice firm and commanding.

Tom played along, feigning innocence. "I'm sorry, Miss Emma. I guess I've just been a bit distracted. I promise I'll do better."

"Promises aren't enough," Emma replied, walking around the desk to stand behind him. She placed a hand on his shoulder, sending a shiver down his spine. "We need to make sure you understand the material."

Emma handed Tom a mock assignment, complete with questions on various subjects. She leaned over him, guiding him through the questions, her proximity and authoritative demeanor heightening the tension between them.

As they progressed, Emma decided to introduce a playful twist. "If you get a question wrong, there will be consequences," she said, her tone playful yet firm.

Tom raised an eyebrow, intrigued. "And what kind of consequences are we talking about, Miss Emma?"

"You'll find out soon enough," she replied, tapping the desk with a ruler for emphasis.

The first few questions went smoothly, but when Tom deliberately answered one incorrectly, Emma's eyes sparkled with mischief. "Incorrect, Mr. Tom. That means you'll need to be disciplined."

Emma stood behind him and gently tapped the ruler against his hand. "Hold out your hand," she instructed. Tom complied, and she lightly tapped his palm with the ruler, their eyes locked in a mixture of amusement and arousal.

As the evening continued, they delved deeper into their roles, the boundaries between their characters and their true selves blurring in the heat of the moment. The playful punishments, the authoritative commands, and the growing tension between them created an electrifying atmosphere.

At one point, Tom couldn't resist any longer. "Miss Emma, I think I need more personal attention to really understand the material," he said, his voice low and suggestive.

Emma, staying in character, replied, "Very well, Mr. Tom. Follow me to my office, and we'll see what we can do."

They moved to the bedroom, which they had previously decided would be the "teacher's office." Emma continued to play her role, now incorporating elements of care and intimacy into their scenario. The evening culminated in a passionate and fulfilling encounter, both of them reveling in the fantasy they had created together.

Afterward, they lay in each other's arms, basking in the afterglow of their shared adventure. They discussed what they enjoyed and how they could improve their role-playing experiences in the future. Their open communication and mutual enjoyment only deepened their bond.

Doctor and Patient: Exploring New Dynamics

The following weekend, Emma and Tom decided to explore another role-playing scenario: doctor and patient. They set the scene in their bedroom, transforming it into a doctor's office with minimal props—a stethoscope, a white lab coat for Emma, and a medical chart.

Emma, now Dr. Emma, adjusted her glasses and picked up the chart as Tom, her patient, entered the room. Tom wore a robe over his clothes, playing the part of someone nervously awaiting a medical examination.

"Mr. Tom, please take a seat," Dr. Emma said, her tone professional and soothing.

Tom sat on the edge of the bed, trying to look convincingly nervous. "Thank you, Dr. Emma. I've been feeling a bit... tense lately."

Dr. Emma nodded sympathetically. "Let's see what we can do about that. I'll need to conduct a thorough examination to determine the cause of your tension."

She began by checking his pulse, her fingers lingering on his wrist longer than necessary. Tom's heart rate quickened, both from the role they were playing and the intimate touch of her hands.

"Your pulse is a bit fast, Mr. Tom. Have you been under a lot of stress recently?" she asked, looking into his eyes with a knowing smile.

Tom nodded. "Yes, Dr. Emma. Work has been quite demanding."

"Well, let's proceed with a more detailed examination," she said, standing behind him and placing the stethoscope against his back. "Take a deep breath for me."

Tom complied, feeling the cool metal of the stethoscope against his skin. Dr. Emma moved the stethoscope to various points on his back, each touch sending a shiver through him.

"Everything sounds normal," she said, putting the stethoscope aside. "But I think a more hands-on approach might help relieve your tension."

Tom's eyes widened with curiosity. "What do you have in mind, Dr. Emma?"

"I'm going to give you a special treatment designed to relax your muscles," she replied, her voice taking on a more intimate tone. She guided him to lie down and began to massage his shoulders and back, her hands firm yet gentle.

As she worked her way down his back, the boundaries between their roles and reality began to blur. The trust and connection they shared made the experience both arousing and deeply intimate.

After the massage, Dr. Emma leaned in close and whispered, "How do you feel now, Mr. Tom?"

Tom turned to face her, his eyes filled with gratitude and desire. "Much better, Dr. Emma. Thank you."

They shared a tender kiss, their role-playing scenario having brought them even closer. The evening ended with them curled up together, discussing their experience and planning future adventures.

In these stories, Emma and Tom explore the dynamics of role-playing through different scenarios, such as teacher-student and doctor-patient. The added conversations bring their characters to life, showcasing the playful yet intimate nature of their interactions. Their experiences highlight the excitement and connection that can come from stepping into different roles, allowing them to explore their fantasies while maintaining a foundation of trust and communication.

A New Experience: Sarah, Jake, and Mia's Threesome Adventure

Sarah and Jake had been together for several years, their relationship marked by trust and open communication. They often discussed their fantasies and desires, creating a safe space to explore their sexuality. One evening, while sharing a bottle of wine, Jake brought up a fantasy he had been thinking about.

"Sarah, I've been wondering how you'd feel about exploring a threesome," Jake said, his voice hesitant but honest. "It's something I've fantasized about, and I'd love to hear your thoughts."

Sarah took a moment to consider his words. She had always appreciated Jake's openness and felt comfortable discussing her own desires. "I'm open to the idea," she replied. "But only if we find someone we both feel comfortable with, and we set clear boundaries."

They decided to take their time finding the right person, discussing their preferences and what they were both comfortable with. After a few months, they met Mia, a mutual friend who they both trusted and found attractive. Mia had expressed interest in joining them, and they all sat down to discuss the details.

"We need to make sure everyone feels safe and respected," Sarah said, looking at both Jake and Mia. "Let's set some ground rules. Communication is key."

Mia nodded in agreement. "Absolutely. We should have a safe word, and if anyone feels uncomfortable at any point, we stop immediately."

With boundaries and consent clearly established, they planned an evening together. Sarah and Jake transformed their bedroom into a cozy and inviting space, with soft lighting and comfortable bedding. They wanted to create an atmosphere where everyone felt at ease.

As the night began, they shared a bottle of wine and relaxed, allowing the conversation to flow naturally. The chemistry between the three of them was undeniable, and soon they found themselves transitioning from conversation to gentle touches and kisses.

Sarah took the lead, guiding the interaction with a combination of confidence and tenderness. She kissed Mia softly, her touch reassuring and gentle. Jake watched, feeling a mix of excitement and gratitude for the trust and connection they all shared.

The evening unfolded with each of them taking turns, ensuring that everyone felt included and appreciated. They communicated openly throughout, checking in with one another and respecting each person's boundaries.

Afterward, they lay together in a tangle of limbs, sharing soft laughter and whispered conversations. The experience had brought them closer, deepening their bond and understanding of each other's desires.

In the days that followed, they continued to communicate openly about their feelings, ensuring that any emotional complexities were addressed. The threesome had been a positive and enriching experience for all of them, rooted in trust, respect, and mutual enjoyment.

An Unexpected Connection: Mark, Lisa, and Rachel's Group Experience

Mark and Lisa had always been adventurous in their relationship, exploring various aspects of their sexuality with enthusiasm and curiosity. One night, while attending a friend's party, they met Rachel, an intriguing woman who shared many of their interests.

As the evening progressed, the three of them found themselves in deep conversation, discussing everything from favorite books to their views on relationships. There was an undeniable chemistry between them, and Mark and Lisa exchanged a knowing glance.

Later, as the party wound down, Mark and Lisa invited Rachel to join them for a nightcap at their apartment. Rachel accepted, feeling a mix of excitement and curiosity. When they arrived, they continued their conversation, but there was a palpable tension in the air.

Lisa decided to break the ice. "Rachel, we've both really enjoyed getting to know you tonight. We've talked about it, and we're interested in exploring a group experience. How do you feel about that?"

Rachel smiled, feeling a rush of excitement. "I've never done anything like this before, but I'm definitely interested. As long as we all communicate and respect each other's boundaries, I'm in."

They spent some time discussing their boundaries and setting ground rules. They agreed on a safe word and emphasized the importance of checking in with each other throughout the experience.

With everything clearly communicated, they moved to the bedroom. The atmosphere was charged with anticipation, but also a sense of mutual respect and understanding. Lisa took the lead, guiding Rachel with gentle touches and reassuring words.

Mark watched, feeling both aroused and deeply connected to Lisa. He joined in, and the three of them navigated their desires with a blend of passion and care. They took turns focusing on each other, ensuring that everyone felt included and appreciated.

The experience was intense and exhilarating, filled with moments of shared pleasure and connection. Afterward, they lay together, basking in the afterglow of their shared adventure.

In the days that followed, Mark and Lisa made sure to communicate openly about their feelings. They checked in with Rachel as well, ensuring that she felt comfortable and respected. The experience had been a positive one, bringing them all closer and adding a new dimension to their relationship.

Through their adventure, Mark, Lisa, and Rachel discovered that group experiences could be deeply fulfilling when approached with clear communication, mutual respect, and a focus on shared pleasure. Their story highlights the importance of trust and understanding in exploring new sexual dynamics.

In these stories, both couples navigate the complexities of engaging in a threesome or group sex scenario with an emphasis on communication, consent, and emotional connection. The added conversations help to illustrate the thoughtful and respectful approach they take, ensuring that the experiences are positive and enriching for all involved.

The Cuckold Fantasy: Exploring the Dynamics of Desire and Trust

A New Understanding: John, Mary, and Kevin's Cuckold Adventure

John and Mary had been married for ten years, their relationship built on a foundation of trust, open communication, and mutual respect. Over time, they had explored various aspects of their sexuality, always ensuring that each new experience was consensual and fulfilling for both of them. Recently, John had been grappling with a fantasy that he found both intriguing and confusing: the idea of Mary being intimate with another man while he watched.

One evening, after a particularly candid conversation about their fantasies, John decided to share his thoughts with Mary. "I've been thinking about something, and I want to talk to you about it," he began, his voice steady but nervous. "I've been fantasizing about you being with another man while I watch. I know it sounds strange, but it's something I can't stop thinking about."

Mary looked at him thoughtfully, appreciating his honesty. "That's definitely an interesting fantasy, John. I want to understand it more. How do you feel about it? What excites you about the idea?"

John took a deep breath. "I think it's about seeing you in a different light, witnessing your pleasure, and feeling a mix of emotions—jealousy, arousal, and excitement. It's a way to explore our boundaries and trust each other even more deeply."

Mary nodded, her mind racing with thoughts. "If we decide to explore this, we need to be very clear about our boundaries and ensure that we're both comfortable. This is a big step, and I want to make sure it strengthens our relationship, not harms it."

They spent the next few weeks discussing the idea, setting clear boundaries, and ensuring that both of them felt comfortable with the potential experience. They agreed that communication and consent were paramount, and they needed to find someone who understood and respected their dynamic.

Eventually, they met Kevin, a friend from Mary's yoga class who they both found trustworthy and open-minded. After a candid discussion about their fantasy and boundaries, Kevin agreed to participate. They set a date for their first experience, each of them feeling a mix of excitement and nervousness.

On the night of their adventure, John transformed their bedroom into a comfortable and inviting space, with soft lighting and soothing music. He wanted to create an atmosphere where everyone felt at ease. Kevin arrived, and the three of them shared a bottle of wine, allowing the conversation to flow naturally.

Mary took the lead, guiding the interaction with a combination of confidence and tenderness. She kissed Kevin softly, her touch reassuring and gentle. John watched, feeling a mix of emotions—arousal, jealousy, excitement—all blending together in a way he had never experienced before.

As the evening unfolded, Mary and Kevin became more intimate, their actions always within the boundaries that had been set. John's heart raced as he watched, feeling a profound sense of connection and trust with Mary. He was captivated by her pleasure, finding a new depth to his feelings for her.

Throughout the experience, they communicated openly, checking in with each other and ensuring that everyone felt comfortable and respected. The trust and connection they shared made the experience both arousing and deeply intimate.

Afterward, they lay together, the three of them sharing soft laughter and whispered conversations. The experience had brought John and Mary closer, deepening their bond and understanding of each other's desires. They thanked Kevin for his participation and openness, ensuring that he felt respected and appreciated.

In the days that followed, John and Mary continued to communicate openly about their feelings, ensuring that any emotional complexities were addressed. The cuckold experience had been a positive and enriching one for both of them, rooted in trust, respect, and mutual enjoyment.

The Unexpected Turn: Alice, Mark, and David's Cuckold Experiment

Alice and Mark had always prided themselves on their adventurous and open-minded relationship. They had explored various fantasies and kinks over the years, each new experience bringing them closer together. Recently, Mark had been entertaining a fantasy that he found both exhilarating and nerve-wracking: the idea of watching Alice with another man.

One evening, after a long and heartfelt conversation about their desires, Mark decided to bring it up. "Alice, I've been thinking about something for a while, and I want to share it with you," he began, his voice filled with both excitement and apprehension. "I've been fantasizing about you being with another man while I watch. It's something that really turns me on, but I want to know how you feel about it."

Alice considered his words carefully. "That's an intriguing fantasy, Mark. I'm open to exploring it, but we need to make sure we're both comfortable and that we communicate clearly. This is a big step, and I want to ensure it's a positive experience for both of us."

They spent the next few weeks discussing the fantasy, setting boundaries, and ensuring that they both felt comfortable with the idea. They agreed that open communication and mutual respect were essential. They also needed to find someone who understood their dynamic and respected their relationship.

They eventually met David, a mutual friend who they both trusted and felt comfortable with. David was intrigued by the idea and agreed to participate, respecting the boundaries and rules that Alice and Mark had set. They planned an evening together, each of them feeling a mix of excitement and nervousness.

On the night of their experiment, Mark set up the living room with comfortable seating and ambient lighting. He wanted to create an environment where everyone felt at ease. David arrived, and the three of them shared drinks and conversation, allowing the tension to build naturally.

Alice took the lead, her confidence and excitement evident in her actions. She kissed David softly, their touch electric. Mark watched, feeling a whirlwind of emotions—jealousy, arousal, and intense excitement. Seeing Alice's pleasure brought him a sense of joy and connection he hadn't anticipated.

As the evening progressed, Alice and David became more intimate, always within the agreed boundaries. Mark's heart raced as he observed, his feelings intensifying with each passing moment. The experience was both arousing and profoundly intimate, deepening his love and trust for Alice.

They communicated openly throughout, ensuring that everyone felt comfortable and respected. The trust and connection they shared made the experience deeply fulfilling.

Afterward, they all relaxed together, sharing laughter and reflecting on the experience. Mark felt a new depth of connection with Alice, their bond strengthened by the trust and openness they had shown each other.

In the days that followed, Alice and Mark continued to communicate about their feelings, ensuring that any emotional complexities were addressed. The cuckold experience had been positive and enriching, bringing them closer and adding a new dimension to their relationship.

In these stories, both couples explore the dynamics of a cuckold fantasy with a focus on communication, consent, and mutual respect. The added conversations help to illustrate the thoughtful and respectful approach they take, ensuring that the experiences are positive and enriching for all involved.

Exploring Boundaries: Emma, James, and Tom's Journey into Openness

Emma and James had always prided themselves on their strong connection and shared sense of adventure. They had explored various aspects of their relationship over the years, from travel to new hobbies, but recently, James had been wrestling with a desire that both intrigued and intimidated him: the idea of opening their relationship to include another man.

One quiet evening, James broached the subject with Emma. "Emma, there's something I've been thinking about," he started, his voice hesitant but earnest. "I've been curious about exploring non-monogamy. The idea of you being with another man while we're both involved—it's something I've fantasized about."

Emma listened carefully, her expression thoughtful. She valued their relationship deeply and knew the importance of open communication. "James, I appreciate you sharing this with me. It's a big step, and I want us to approach it thoughtfully. Let's talk more about what this could look like and how we both feel about it."

Over the following weeks, Emma and James had many conversations, exploring their boundaries, fears, and desires. They agreed that any exploration would be rooted in honesty, respect, and clear communication. They also discussed the importance of finding someone they both trusted and who understood their relationship dynamic.

They eventually met Tom, a friend who had always been respectful and supportive of their relationship. Tom was intrigued by the idea and willing to explore with them under the boundaries they had set. They planned a night together, feeling a mixture of excitement and nervousness.

On the agreed-upon evening, James and Emma prepared their home, creating a comfortable and welcoming space for their exploration. When Tom arrived, they shared a relaxed dinner, allowing the evening to unfold naturally. There was an undercurrent of anticipation as they shared stories and laughter, easing into the intimacy of the moment.

Emma took the lead, her confidence and desire evident as she kissed Tom softly, her touch gentle yet charged with electricity. James watched, his emotions swirling—a blend of excitement, insecurity, and a surprising sense of compersion, feeling a deep happiness in seeing Emma's pleasure.

As the night progressed, Emma, James, and Tom navigated new territory together, always respecting the boundaries they had set. James found himself surprised by the complexity of his emotions—moments of jealousy were quickly replaced by waves of arousal and a profound connection to Emma.

Throughout the experience, they communicated openly and honestly, ensuring that everyone felt comfortable and respected. They paused when needed to check in with each other, reaffirming their trust and deepening their bond through shared vulnerability.

Afterward, they cuddled together, basking in the afterglow and sharing quiet moments of reflection. James felt a new closeness with Emma, their bond strengthened by the trust and mutual respect they had shown each other.

In the days that followed, Emma and James continued to talk about their experience, addressing any lingering emotions or questions that arose. They found that the exploration had deepened their intimacy and brought them closer, reaffirming their commitment to each other and their shared journey of growth and discovery.

This story illustrates a journey of exploration and trust, highlighting the complexities and emotional richness that can arise when couples navigate new dimensions of their relationship together.

Embracing Desire: Sarah, Michael, and Adam's Journey of Discovery

Sarah and Michael had been married for over a decade, their bond strengthened by mutual respect, trust, and a shared love for adventure. They had always been open about their fantasies and desires, and recently, Michael had been harboring a fantasy that intrigued him deeply: the idea of Sarah exploring intimacy with another man while he watched.

One quiet evening, Michael decided to share his thoughts with Sarah. "Sarah, there's something I've been thinking about," he began, his voice tinged with nervous excitement. "I've been curious about seeing you with another man. The idea of sharing that experience with you—it's something that excites me, but I want to know how you feel about it."

Sarah listened attentively, her heart racing with a mix of surprise and curiosity. She valued their relationship and knew that open communication was key. "Michael, I appreciate you being honest with me about this," she replied thoughtfully. "It's a lot to consider, but I'm open to exploring it with you. Let's talk more about what this could look like and how we both feel."

Over the following weeks, Sarah and Michael had many heartfelt discussions, exploring their boundaries, fears, and desires. They agreed that any exploration would be rooted in trust, respect, and ongoing communication. They also discussed the importance of finding someone they both trusted and who understood the significance of their relationship.

They eventually connected with Adam, a friend who had always been supportive and respectful of their marriage. Adam was intrigued by the idea and willing to participate under the guidelines they had set. They planned a special evening together, a mix of anticipation and nervous excitement filling the air.

On the chosen night, Sarah and Michael prepared their home, creating a warm and inviting atmosphere for their exploration. When Adam arrived, they shared a relaxed dinner, the conversation flowing naturally as they eased into the evening.

Sarah initiated the first move, her confidence and desire evident as she kissed Adam gently, her touch tender yet filled with longing. Michael watched intently, a rush of emotions washing over him—excitement, nervousness, and a surprising sense of compersion, feeling deep happiness in seeing Sarah explore her desires.

As the night progressed, Sarah, Michael, and Adam navigated new territory together, always mindful of the boundaries they had set. Michael found himself surprised by the complexity of his emotions—brief moments of jealousy giving way to waves of arousal and an unexpected sense of intimacy with Sarah.

Throughout the experience, they communicated openly and honestly, ensuring that everyone felt comfortable and respected. They paused to check in with each other, reaffirming their trust and deepening their connection through shared vulnerability.

Afterward, they cuddled together, basking in the afterglow and sharing quiet moments of reflection. Michael felt a newfound closeness with Sarah, their bond strengthened by the trust and mutual respect they had shown each other.

In the days that followed, Sarah and Michael continued to discuss their experience, addressing any lingering emotions or questions that arose. They found that exploring this new dimension of their relationship had deepened their intimacy and brought them even closer, reaffirming their love and commitment to each other.

This story explores the journey of Sarah, Michael, and Adam as they navigate new desires and boundaries in their relationship, highlighting the power of trust, communication, and mutual exploration.

A Shared Journey: Emily, Jack, and Ryan's Exploration of Openness

Emily and Jack had been together for several years, their relationship built on a foundation of trust, respect, and a shared sense of adventure. They had always been open about their fantasies and desires, and recently, Jack had expressed an interest in exploring non-monogamy—a desire that both excited and challenged them.

One evening, Jack decided to broach the subject with Emily. "Emily, there's something I've been thinking about," he started cautiously, his heart racing with anticipation. "I've been curious about exploring intimacy with other people while still being committed to you. It's something that I believe could strengthen our connection, but I want to know how you feel about it."

Emily listened attentively, her mind racing with a mix of emotions—surprise, curiosity, and a deep desire to understand Jack's perspective. She valued their relationship deeply and knew that open communication was essential. "Jack, I appreciate you sharing this with me," she replied thoughtfully. "It's a lot to take in, but I'm open to exploring it with you. Let's talk more about what this could look like and how we can approach it together."

Over the following weeks, Emily and Jack engaged in numerous heartfelt conversations, exploring their boundaries, fears, and hopes for the future. They agreed that any exploration would be grounded in mutual respect, honesty, and ongoing communication. They also discussed the importance of finding partners who respected their relationship and understood the significance of their commitment to each other.

They eventually connected with Ryan, a friend from Jack's social circle who had always shown respect for their relationship. Ryan was intrigued by the idea and willing to participate under the guidelines they had established. They planned a special weekend together, a mix of excitement and nervous anticipation filling the air.

On the chosen weekend, Emily and Jack prepared their home, creating a welcoming and comfortable environment for their exploration. When Ryan arrived, they shared a relaxed evening, the conversation flowing naturally as they enjoyed each other's company.

Emily initiated the first move, her confidence and desire palpable as she kissed Ryan softly, her touch filled with both tenderness and longing. Jack observed with a mixture of emotions—curiosity, excitement, and a profound sense of compersion, feeling a deep joy in seeing Emily explore her desires in a safe and respectful manner.

As the weekend unfolded, Emily, Jack, and Ryan navigated new experiences together, always mindful of the boundaries they had set. Jack found himself surprised by the depth of his emotions—brief moments of uncertainty giving way to waves of admiration and an unexpected sense of connection with Emily.

Throughout their time together, they communicated openly and honestly, ensuring that everyone felt comfortable and respected. They checked in with each other regularly, reaffirming their trust and strengthening their bond through shared vulnerability and mutual exploration.

Afterward, they spent time together, enjoying moments of closeness and reflection. Emily and Jack felt a renewed sense of intimacy and connection, their love for each other deepened by the trust and openness they had shared.

In the days that followed, Emily and Jack continued to discuss their experiences and emotions, addressing any lingering questions or concerns that arose. They found that exploring this new aspect of their relationship had not only strengthened their bond but had also enriched their understanding of themselves and each other.

This story showcases the journey of Emily, Jack, and Ryan as they navigate new desires and boundaries in their relationship, highlighting the importance of trust, communication, and mutual exploration.

Advice on Why Men Agree to Cuckolding Dynamics

1. Exploration of Deep Fantasies

Many men agree to cuckolding because it allows them to explore deep-seated fantasies. For John, watching Mary with Kevin brought his fantasies to life, letting him experience a mixture of emotions—arousal, jealousy, and excitement. Acknowledging and exploring such fantasies can lead to a greater understanding of oneself and one's desires.

2. Voyeuristic Pleasure

For men like Mark, the visual and emotional aspects of seeing their partner with someone else can be incredibly arousing. The act of watching, combined with the trust placed in the partner, heightens the overall experience. This voyeuristic pleasure can be a powerful motivator in agreeing to cuckolding dynamics.

3. Enhanced Emotional Intimacy

Cuckolding can deepen the emotional bond between partners. In both stories, the couples communicated openly about their feelings and boundaries, which strengthened their relationship. For men like Tom, knowing Sarah was with another man and being involved in the process brought them closer together, enhancing their emotional intimacy.

4. Trust and Connection

Engaging in cuckolding requires a high level of trust and communication between partners. Men who agree to this dynamic often do so to build and test the strength of their relationship. By trusting their partner to respect boundaries and communicate openly, they create a deeper connection and mutual respect.

5. Embracing Vulnerability

Cuckolding can be a way for men to embrace vulnerability and explore their emotions. Feeling jealousy, excitement, and arousal simultaneously can lead to personal growth and a better understanding of one's emotional landscape. This vulnerability, when shared with a partner, can foster a stronger, more intimate bond.

6. Fetish or Fantasy Fulfillment

For some men, the desire to see their partner with another person is a specific fetish or fantasy. Acting on this fantasy within a consensual and controlled environment allows them to fulfill their desires in a safe and respectful manner. This fulfillment can bring a sense of satisfaction and completeness to their sexual life.

7. Experiencing Compersion

Compersion, the feeling of joy from seeing one's partner happy and pleasured by someone else, can be a significant motivator. For men like John, witnessing Mary's pleasure with Kevin brought him happiness and satisfaction. Embracing compersion can enhance emotional bonds and contribute to a positive experience.

8. Safe Exploration of Power Dynamics

Cuckolding allows men to explore power dynamics in their relationship. Whether it's a feeling of submission, dominance, or equal partnership, these dynamics can add a layer of complexity and excitement to the relationship. Understanding and navigating these dynamics safely and consensually can lead to a more fulfilling sexual and emotional connection.

Conclusion

Men may agree to cuckolding for various reasons, including the exploration of fantasies, voyeuristic pleasure, enhanced emotional intimacy, trust-building, embracing vulnerability, fetish fulfillment, experiencing compression, and safe exploration of power dynamics. The key to a positive cuckolding experience lies in open communication, mutual respect, and clear boundaries. By fostering an environment of trust and understanding, couples can explore this dynamic in a way that enriches their relationship and deepens their connection.

This advice is rooted in the experiences of the couples in the stories, emphasizing the importance of communication, trust, and mutual respect in exploring cuckolding dynamics.

Chapter 3: Lack of Emotional Attachment

Some men might tolerate or even find fulfillment in cuckolding dynamics due to a lack of emotional attachment to traditional notions of sexual exclusivity and monogamy. This perspective can influence their approach to relationships in several ways:

1. Separation of Sex and Emotions

For some men, sex and emotions are distinct aspects of a relationship. They might view sexual activities as separate from their emotional bond with their partner. This separation allows them to engage in or tolerate cuckolding without feeling that it threatens their primary emotional connection.

2. Focus on Personal Fulfillment

A lack of emotional attachment to traditional norms can lead to a greater focus on personal and mutual fulfillment. Men who agree to cuckolding may prioritize their own and their partner's sexual satisfaction over adhering to conventional expectations. This approach allows both partners to explore their desires more freely.

3. Acceptance of Diverse Desires

Men with less emotional attachment to traditional relationship norms often have a greater acceptance of diverse desires and fantasies. They recognize that their partner's sexual interests may differ from their own and are more open to exploring these differences in a consensual and supportive manner.

4. Reduced Jealousy

Lack of emotional attachment to traditional norms can result in reduced feelings of jealousy. Men who are not emotionally invested in the idea of sexual exclusivity might find it easier to accept and even enjoy their partner's sexual experiences with others. This reduced jealousy can create a more harmonious and open relationship dynamic.

5. Enhanced Communication

Men who lack emotional attachment to traditional norms often engage in more open and honest communication with their partners. They discuss their boundaries, desires, and expectations more freely, leading to a stronger and more transparent relationship. This communication helps to ensure that both partners feel respected and understood.

6. Embracing Non-Traditional Dynamics

For some men, a lack of emotional attachment to traditional norms means they are more comfortable embracing non-traditional relationship dynamics. They might find that cuckolding aligns better with their personal beliefs and values, allowing them to create a relationship that feels more authentic and fulfilling.

7. Increased Trust and Intimacy

Paradoxically, a lack of emotional attachment to traditional norms can lead to increased trust and intimacy. By openly discussing and exploring their desires, men and their partners build a foundation of trust that goes beyond conventional expectations. This deeper level of trust can enhance their overall emotional connection.

8. Respecting Partner's Autonomy

Men who are less emotionally attached to traditional norms often have a greater respect for their partner's autonomy. They support their partner's right to explore their own desires and needs, viewing this autonomy as a key component of a healthy and respectful relationship.

9. Exploration of Fantasies

A lack of emotional attachment to traditional norms can encourage the exploration of fantasies that might otherwise be suppressed. Men who engage in cuckolding might do so because it allows them to explore their own and their partner's fantasies in a safe and consensual environment. This exploration can lead to greater sexual satisfaction and personal growth.

10. Flexibility in Relationship Roles

Men who are less emotionally attached to traditional norms are often more flexible in their relationship roles. They are open to redefining their roles and responsibilities within the relationship, creating a dynamic that is more adaptable and responsive to their changing needs and desires.

Conclusion

A lack of emotional attachment to traditional relationship norms can influence why some men agree to and find fulfillment in cuckolding dynamics. By separating sex and emotions, focusing on personal fulfillment, accepting diverse desires, reducing jealousy, enhancing communication, embracing non-traditional dynamics, increasing trust and intimacy, respecting their partner's autonomy, exploring fantasies, and maintaining flexibility in relationship roles, they create a relationship that is more authentic, fulfilling, and respectful of both partners' needs and desires. This approach allows them to navigate cuckolding dynamics in a way that strengthens their emotional and sexual connection.

Journey Through Emotional Detachment: A Woman's Perspective

I've always found it challenging to form deep emotional connections in my relationships. It's not that I don't crave intimacy or care deeply for my partners, but there's this lingering sense of detachment that I can't seem to shake off.

In my last relationship, I was with someone who was kind, supportive, and genuinely cared for me. We shared interests, had great conversations, and enjoyed each other's company. On paper, everything seemed perfect. Yet, deep down, I couldn't fully immerse myself emotionally. It's like there's a barrier preventing me from letting my guard down completely.

I've reflected on this aspect of myself a lot. I've come to realize that it's not about my partners or their actions—it's more about my own internal struggles with vulnerability and trust. Growing up, I witnessed relationships around me that were tumultuous and emotionally draining. I think subconsciously, I built walls to protect myself from experiencing similar pain.

This lack of emotional attachment doesn't mean I don't value or appreciate my partners. I do. I cherish the moments we share and the connections we form. However, when things start to get too intense or demanding emotionally, I find myself retreating into a space where I can maintain a sense of control and independence.

It's been a journey of self-discovery and acceptance. I've learned to communicate my feelings honestly with my partners, explaining that my struggle with emotional attachment is not a reflection of them or their worth. I've also sought therapy to work through my internal barriers and develop healthier ways of connecting with others.

Navigating relationships with this lack of emotional attachment has its challenges. There are times when I feel guilty for not reciprocating my partner's deep emotional investment. But I've come to understand that everyone experiences love and connection differently, and my journey is just as valid.

Moving forward, I hope to continue exploring ways to cultivate deeper emotional connections while honoring my need for personal autonomy and self-protection. It's a delicate balance, but I'm committed to growing and evolving in my relationships, finding fulfillment in my own unique way.

This testimony provides insight into the complexities of experiencing a lack of emotional attachment in relationships, highlighting personal growth, self-awareness, and the journey towards understanding and acceptance.

Emotional Distance: A Man's Journey in Relationships

I've always found myself struggling to connect deeply with others on an emotional level. It's not that I don't care or want to be close to someone, but there's this barrier that I can't seem to break through.

In my past relationships, I've had partners who were wonderful people—kind, caring, and supportive. They would open up to me, sharing their hopes, dreams, and fears, while I listened attentively and offered my support. Yet, despite their openness, I found myself unable to reciprocate in the same way.

I think part of it stems from my own upbringing. I grew up in a family where emotions were rarely expressed openly. My parents were loving but reserved, and I learned early on to keep my feelings to myself. Over time, this became my default mode of operating in relationships—keeping a safe distance emotionally to avoid vulnerability.

I've had moments where I've questioned myself, wondering if there's something wrong with me or if I'm incapable of love. But deep down, I know it's more about my fear of being hurt or disappointing others. I've seen how intense emotions can lead to conflict and heartache, and I guess I've developed a protective mechanism to shield myself from that pain.

It's not that I don't value my partners or appreciate their love and affection. I do, deeply. I enjoy spending time with them, sharing experiences, and building memories together. But when things start to get too emotionally intense, I find myself pulling back, creating space to maintain a sense of control and independence.

I've tried to be honest with my partners about my struggles with emotional attachment. I've explained that it's not a reflection of their worth or our relationship—it's more about my own internal battles with vulnerability and trust. Some have understood and been patient with me, while others have found it difficult to accept.

Navigating relationships with this lack of emotional attachment has been challenging. There have been moments of guilt and self-doubt, wondering if I'm capable of giving and receiving love in the way my partners deserve. But I'm committed to understanding myself better and exploring ways to cultivate deeper emotional connections, while also respecting my need for personal autonomy and self-protection.

I'm hopeful that with time and self-reflection, I'll be able to break down the walls I've built around my heart and experience the kind of love and intimacy that I know is possible.

This testimony provides insight into the complexities of experiencing a lack of emotional attachment in relationships from a man's perspective, highlighting personal introspection, challenges, and a journey towards understanding and growth.

Casual Relationship Dynamics

In casual or less emotionally invested relationships, fidelity and exclusivity often take on different meanings and priorities compared to more traditional or committed partnerships. Here's a deeper exploration of how these dynamics influence some men's attitudes towards fidelity:

1. **Emphasis on Enjoyment and Freedom**: In casual relationships, individuals often prioritize enjoyment and personal freedom. This can mean less emphasis on strict fidelity and more openness to exploring connections with others.
2. **Defined Boundaries**: While fidelity might not be a central concern, clarity in communication about boundaries is crucial. Men in casual relationships may establish what is acceptable and what isn't, ensuring both parties are comfortable and respected.
3. **Exploration and Variety**: Casual relationships can provide a platform for exploring different aspects of one's sexuality and preferences. Men may be more inclined to engage in non-exclusive arrangements to satisfy their curiosity or desire for variety.
4. **Less Emotional Investment**: Compared to committed relationships, casual partnerships may involve less emotional investment. This can translate into a lower priority placed on exclusivity, with the focus remaining on enjoying the present moment rather than long-term fidelity.
5. **Mutual Understanding**: Successful casual relationships often hinge on mutual understanding and respect. Men who participate in these dynamics typically value open communication and honesty to maintain harmony and avoid misunderstandings.
6. **Personal Growth and Independence**: For some men, casual relationships represent a period of personal growth and independence. They may see non-monogamous arrangements as conducive to exploring their own needs and desires without the constraints of traditional relationship expectations.
7. **Adaptability and Flexibility**: Casual relationships offer a level of adaptability and flexibility that can appeal to men seeking less rigid relationship structures. This adaptability allows for fluidity in defining boundaries and exploring different dynamics as circumstances evolve.
8. **Challenges and Considerations**: Despite the freedom casual relationships offer, challenges like jealousy or misunderstandings can still arise. Effective communication and mutual respect are essential for navigating these challenges and maintaining healthy connections.

In summary, men in casual relationships may approach fidelity and exclusivity differently, prioritizing enjoyment, freedom, and clear communication. These relationships provide opportunities for exploration, personal growth, and a flexible approach to defining relationship boundaries.

Embracing Freedom: Sarah's Journey in a Casual Relationship

Sarah had always been drawn to the thrill of spontaneity and the freedom to explore life on her terms. At 28, she found herself immersed in a casual relationship with Mark, a charming and ambitious colleague. Their connection was electric, fueled by shared interests and a mutual understanding of their non-committal arrangement.

For Sarah, the appeal lay in the uncomplicated nature of their dynamic. She cherished the evenings spent together—carefree dinners, adventurous outings, and intimate conversations that flowed effortlessly. Mark understood her desire for independence and respected her need for personal space, traits that Sarah found refreshing after years of more traditional relationships.

In their casual relationship, fidelity didn't hold the same weight as it had in Sarah's past. They were open about their expectations from the start, setting clear boundaries that allowed them to enjoy each other's company without the pressure of exclusivity. This openness fostered a sense of trust between them, a crucial foundation in navigating their arrangement.

As weeks turned into months, Sarah found herself appreciating the simplicity and authenticity of their connection. She felt free to pursue her career goals and personal passions without the constraints of a committed partnership. Yet, beneath the surface, she began to wonder about the potential for deeper emotional intimacy—something she hadn't anticipated in a casual setting.

Their relationship posed its challenges too. Moments of jealousy occasionally crept in, reminders of the blurred lines between casual companionship and emotional attachment. Yet, through honest communication and mutual respect, Sarah and Mark navigated these challenges together, strengthening their bond and reaffirming their individual priorities.

Sarah's journey in this casual relationship was a reflection of her evolving understanding of love and companionship. It taught her to value the present moment, embrace her independence, and cherish the connections that enriched her life, regardless of their form.

This story portrays Sarah's experience in a casual relationship, highlighting themes of independence, mutual respect, and the complexities of navigating emotions in a non-committal setting.

Exploring Connection: James' Journey in a Casual Relationship

James had always been focused on his career and personal growth, relishing the independence that came with being single in his late twenties. His casual relationship with Emily, a fellow art enthusiast he met at a gallery opening, seemed like a perfect fit for his lifestyle at the time.

Their connection was magnetic yet laid-back, characterized by spontaneous dates exploring new restaurants, hiking trails, and attending local events together. James appreciated Emily's adventurous spirit and admired her dedication to her artistic pursuits. They shared a mutual understanding from the outset that theirs was not a relationship bound by traditional expectations.

For James, the appeal of their arrangement lay in its flexibility and lack of pressure. He valued the freedom to focus on his career ambitions without feeling guilty about neglecting a partner's needs. Emily, too, valued her independence and found solace in knowing James supported her artistic endeavors without the constraints of a committed relationship.

Their casual relationship allowed them both to explore their individual interests while enjoying the companionship and intimacy they craved. They communicated openly about their boundaries and expectations, ensuring they were always on the same page despite the non-committal nature of their connection.

As time passed, James found himself contemplating the deeper emotional connection he shared with Emily. Their bond, initially based on shared interests and mutual respect, began to evolve as they navigated challenges together and supported each other through personal milestones.

However, James also faced moments of introspection and occasional bouts of uncertainty. He wondered if their casual relationship could evolve into something more meaningful or if their differing life priorities would eventually lead them down separate paths.

Through honest conversations and mutual understanding, James and Emily continued to explore their connection, embracing the present moment while remaining open to whatever the future might hold. Their journey in this casual relationship taught James valuable lessons about love, companionship, and the importance of embracing personal growth alongside romantic pursuits.

This story depicts James' experience in a casual relationship, highlighting themes of independence, personal growth, and navigating emotions in a non-traditional partnership.

Yearning for More: Emily's Journey in a Casual Relationship

Emily had always valued her independence and cherished the freedom to pursue her passions without the constraints of a committed relationship. When she met Adam at a friend's party, there was an instant connection—a spark that ignited shared laughter, deep conversations, and spontaneous adventures around the city.

Their casual relationship began with excitement and a mutual understanding of their non-committal arrangement. Emily enjoyed Adam's company immensely—they shared similar interests in music, art, and exploring new cuisines. They spent weekends together, enjoying each other's presence without the pressure of defining their relationship.

However, as months passed, Emily started feeling a sense of unease creeping into her heart. Despite their agreement to keep things casual, she found herself yearning for more emotional intimacy and connection. Adam remained true to their arrangement, prioritizing his career and personal freedom over deeper commitment.

Emily's sadness grew as she realized the limitations of their relationship. She longed for someone to share her hopes, dreams, and vulnerabilities—a partner who would be there for her through life's challenges and celebrations. Yet, every time she considered broaching the topic with Adam, fear of rejection and disrupting their current dynamic held her back.

She began questioning her own desires and wondering if she was asking for too much. She felt torn between honoring her need for emotional fulfillment and respecting Adam's desire for autonomy. The ambiguity of their relationship left her feeling emotionally drained and uncertain about her future.

Despite their shared moments of joy and connection, Emily couldn't shake the sadness that accompanied their casual arrangement. She yearned for clarity and a sense of direction, longing to find someone who could meet her emotional needs and share a deeper bond beyond surface-level interactions.

As she navigated her feelings, Emily realized the importance of valuing herself and her emotional well-being. She knew she deserved a relationship where her feelings were reciprocated and her heart felt secure. With a heavy heart, Emily made the difficult decision to express her feelings to Adam, knowing that it might lead to a change in their dynamic or even the end of their relationship.

This story reflects the emotional complexities and challenges that can arise from being in a casual relationship, highlighting the sadness and longing for deeper connection from a woman's perspective.

Navigating Casual Waters: A Tale of Heartache in the Office

In the bustling offices of a multinational corporation, Adam found himself caught in a whirlwind of deadlines, meetings, and the constant hum of productivity. As a driven project manager with ambitions to climb the corporate ladder, he thrived on the challenges that came with overseeing complex initiatives and leading a team of dedicated professionals.

Amidst the controlled chaos of his professional life, Adam's personal life took an unexpected turn when he became romantically involved with Sarah, a talented graphic designer known for her creativity and infectious laughter. Their casual relationship began innocently enough, sparked by shared lunches in the office cafeteria and occasional after-work drinks with colleagues.

At first, Adam relished the simplicity of their arrangement—a welcome contrast to the high-pressure environment of his job. He appreciated Sarah's easygoing nature and the way she effortlessly brought levity to their interactions. Yet, as weeks turned into months, Adam began to feel a growing sense of sadness and uncertainty creeping into his heart.

Their relationship, defined by its casual nature, left Adam yearning for deeper emotional connection and intimacy. He found himself drawn to Sarah's warmth and intelligence, craving moments of closeness beyond the confines of their office interactions. However, Sarah remained steadfast in her commitment to keeping things light and uncomplicated, prioritizing her independence and career aspirations.

As they navigated the complexities of their relationship within the office environment, Adam struggled with conflicting emotions. He felt a deepening sense of sadness as he realized that their connection, while fulfilling in some ways, lacked the emotional depth and commitment he desired. Their shared moments of laughter and camaraderie in the workplace served as bittersweet reminders of what could have been.

In quiet moments at his desk, Adam wrestled with his feelings of longing and resignation. He questioned whether he was asking too much or if he deserved more from their relationship. The blurred lines between professional and personal life added an additional layer of complexity, as Adam grappled with maintaining professionalism while navigating the complexities of his emotions.

Despite their best efforts to maintain boundaries and uphold their professional reputations, Adam couldn't shake the sadness that accompanied their casual arrangement. He yearned for clarity and a sense of direction, longing to find someone who could meet his emotional needs and share a deeper bond beyond fleeting moments in the office.

As he continued to navigate the intricacies of office politics and personal desires, Adam learned valuable lessons about boundaries, emotional resilience, and the importance of prioritizing his own happiness and well-being in both his professional and personal life.

This story delves into the emotional challenges faced by Adam in a casual relationship within an office setting, highlighting the complexities of balancing personal desires with professional responsibilities.

Finding Faith, Losing Love: A Man's Journey of Heartache in the Church

In the serene halls of St. Mary's Parish, Daniel found solace amidst the stained glass windows and the hushed whispers of prayers echoing through the sanctuary. As a devout member of the church community, he dedicated himself to his faith and found fulfillment in serving others through volunteer work and spiritual guidance.

Amidst his dedication to the church, Daniel's personal life took an unexpected turn when he crossed paths with Anna, a fellow parishioner known for her kindness and unwavering devotion to her faith. Their casual relationship began innocently enough, sparked by shared moments during church events and bible study groups.

At first, Daniel appreciated the simplicity of their arrangement—a welcome respite from the complexities of modern dating. He admired Anna's compassion and deep-rooted faith, finding comfort in their shared beliefs and discussions about spirituality. Yet, as their connection deepened, Daniel began to feel a growing sense of sadness and unease creeping into his heart.

Their relationship, defined by its casual nature, left Daniel yearning for deeper emotional connection and commitment. He found himself drawn to Anna's gentle spirit and the way she radiated warmth and kindness within the church community. However, Anna remained steadfast in her commitment to keeping things platonic and maintaining a focus on their shared faith.

As they navigated the complexities of their relationship within the church environment, Daniel struggled with conflicting emotions. He felt a deepening sense of sadness as he realized that their connection, while spiritually enriching, lacked the emotional depth and intimacy he desired. Their shared moments of worship and fellowship served as poignant reminders of what could have been.

In moments of quiet reflection within the church pews, Daniel wrestled with his feelings of longing and resignation. He questioned whether he was asking too much or if he deserved more from their relationship. The sanctity of the church added an additional layer of complexity, as Daniel grappled with maintaining his faith while navigating the complexities of his emotions.

Despite their shared commitment to faith and shared values, Daniel couldn't shake the sadness that accompanied their casual arrangement. He yearned for clarity and a sense of direction, longing to find someone who could meet his emotional needs and share a deeper bond beyond their spiritual connection.

As he continued to seek solace in his faith and navigate the intricacies of church life, Daniel learned valuable lessons about resilience, self-discovery, and the importance of prioritizing his own emotional well-being. His journey of heartache within the church community ultimately led him to a deeper understanding of faith, love, and the complexities of human relationships.

This story explores the emotional challenges faced by Daniel in a casual relationship within the context of a church setting, highlighting the conflicts between spiritual devotion and personal desires.

Lessons in Heartache: A Woman's Journey of Sadness in a Casual Relationship

In the halls of Ridgeview High School, where laughter echoed between classes and friendships blossomed amidst the chaos of teenage life, Mia found herself navigating the complexities of a casual relationship with Jake, a charming and popular senior known for his easy smile and charismatic demeanor.

Their relationship began innocently enough, sparked by shared classes and mutual friends. Mia was drawn to Jake's confidence and sense of adventure, while Jake admired Mia's intelligence and artistic talents. They spent lunch breaks together, swapping stories and dreams for the future, their bond deepening with each passing day.

At first, Mia relished the simplicity of their arrangement—a welcomed break from the pressures of academics and teenage drama. She appreciated Jake's company and the way he made her feel special during their stolen moments between classes and extracurricular activities. Yet, as their connection evolved, Mia began to feel a growing sense of sadness and longing creeping into her heart.

Their relationship, defined by its casual nature, left Mia yearning for more emotional intimacy and commitment. She found herself drawn to Jake's magnetic personality and the way he made her laugh, yet struggled with the uncertainty of where their relationship was headed. Jake, focused on his upcoming graduation and future plans, remained non-committal, prioritizing his freedom and friendships over a deeper emotional connection.

As they navigated the complexities of their relationship within the school environment, Mia wrestled with conflicting emotions. She felt a deepening sense of sadness as she realized that their connection, while exciting and fun, lacked the emotional depth and security she desired. Their shared moments in the school hallways and at weekend parties served as bittersweet reminders of what could have been.

In moments of solitude in the school library or during quiet study sessions, Mia reflected on her feelings of longing and resignation. She questioned whether she was asking for too much or if she deserved more from their relationship. The academic pressures and social dynamics of high school added an additional layer of complexity, as Mia grappled with maintaining her grades while navigating the complexities of her emotions.

Despite their shared laughter and moments of camaraderie, Mia couldn't shake the sadness that accompanied their casual arrangement. She yearned for clarity and a sense of direction, longing to find someone who could meet her emotional needs and share a deeper bond beyond fleeting moments in the school corridors.

As she continued to navigate the challenges of teenage life and personal growth, Mia learned valuable lessons about self-worth, resilience, and the importance of prioritizing her own happiness and emotional well-being. Her journey through heartache within the school community ultimately led her to a deeper understanding of love, friendship, and the complexities of navigating relationships during adolescence.

This story explores the emotional challenges faced by Mia in a casual relationship within the setting of a school, highlighting the conflicts between teenage desires for connection and the realities of casual arrangements.

Understanding Emotional Detachment in Relationships

Emotional detachment in relationships refers to a state where individuals maintain a certain level of distance or lack of emotional investment in their romantic partners. This detachment can manifest in various ways, including prioritizing other aspects of the relationship, such as friendship, companionship, or practical considerations, over exclusivity and emotional intimacy.

Factors Contributing to Emotional Detachment:

1. **Fear of Vulnerability:** Some individuals may have a fear of being emotionally vulnerable or getting hurt. As a result, they consciously or unconsciously maintain emotional distance to protect themselves from potential pain or disappointment.
2. **Past Experiences:** Previous relationships or childhood experiences can shape one's ability to form deep emotional connections. Traumatic experiences, abandonment issues, or witnessing dysfunctional relationships can lead individuals to develop coping mechanisms that involve emotional detachment.

3. **Desire for Independence:** People who highly value their independence and personal autonomy may prioritize their freedom over emotional dependence on a partner. They may prefer relationships that offer companionship and support without the expectation of exclusivity or intense emotional involvement.
4. **Communication Styles:** Differences in communication styles and emotional expression can also contribute to emotional detachment. Some individuals may find it challenging to articulate their feelings or connect emotionally with their partners, leading to a sense of distance in the relationship.

Impact on Attitudes Towards Infidelity:

Emotional detachment can influence how individuals perceive and respond to infidelity within their relationships:

- **Permissive Attitudes:** In relationships where emotional detachment is prevalent, partners may be more tolerant or accepting of infidelity. Since emotional intimacy and exclusivity are not primary factors, the emphasis may be on other aspects of the relationship, such as practical arrangements or companionship.

- **Lack of Emotional Investment:** A lack of emotional investment can lead to partners viewing infidelity as less damaging or threatening to the relationship. They may rationalize infidelity as a separate aspect of their partner's behavior that does not directly impact the emotional bond or companionship they share.

- **Conflict Avoidance:** Emotional detachment can also result in avoiding confrontations or emotional discussions about infidelity. Partners may choose to overlook or downplay instances of infidelity to maintain the stability and practical benefits of the relationship.

Challenges and Considerations:

- **Emotional Fulfillment:** While emotional detachment may offer a sense of independence and autonomy, it can also result in feelings of loneliness or dissatisfaction. Partners may miss out on the deep emotional connection and intimacy that can enhance relationship satisfaction and personal well-being.

- **Communication and Understanding:** Open communication and mutual understanding are essential in navigating relationships with emotional detachment. Partners should discuss their expectations, boundaries, and feelings openly to ensure that both parties are on the same page regarding the nature and dynamics of the relationship.

- **Personal Growth:** Individuals experiencing emotional detachment may benefit from self-reflection and exploration of their emotional needs and relationship patterns. Seeking support from trusted friends, family, or a therapist can help in developing healthier ways of connecting with others and fostering more fulfilling relationships.

In summary, emotional detachment in relationships can lead to a more permissive attitude towards infidelity, as partners prioritize aspects such as companionship or practical arrangements over emotional exclusivity. Understanding the underlying factors and communicating openly about expectations and boundaries are crucial in navigating relationships where emotional detachment plays a significant role.

Testimony of Mark, 34 years old:

"Growing up, I saw my parents struggle with their emotions and often witnessed their conflicts escalate due to misunderstandings and unmet expectations. As a result, I developed a subconscious fear of getting too emotionally involved

in relationships. When I met Sarah, I was immediately drawn to her warmth and intelligence. We connected on many levels, but I found myself holding back emotionally. Sarah was patient and understanding, but I struggled to express my deepest feelings and fears. Over time, this emotional detachment became a barrier between us. I yearned for connection but couldn't overcome my fear of vulnerability. It's been a journey of self-discovery and learning to navigate my emotions, but I realize now the importance of addressing my fears to build healthier relationships."

Testimony of Emily, 30 years old:

"I've always valued my independence and personal space, even in relationships. When I met Alex, I admired his ambition and kindness. We enjoyed each other's company and shared many interests, but I found myself hesitant to fully commit emotionally. For me, relationships were about companionship and shared experiences rather than deep emotional bonds. Alex wanted more, but I struggled to meet his expectations. It was difficult to explain that my detachment wasn't about him—it was about my own need for autonomy and fear of losing myself in a relationship. Our relationship taught me that while I cherish companionship, I need to find a balance that respects my emotional boundaries and allows for mutual understanding."

Testimony of James, 28 years old:

"Growing up in a household where emotions were rarely discussed, I learned to keep my feelings guarded. When I met Laura, I was captivated by her wit and charm. We enjoyed spending time together and shared many interests, but I struggled to express my emotions fully. Laura wanted intimacy and emotional connection, but I found myself withdrawing whenever things became too intense. It wasn't that I didn't care for her—I did deeply—but I feared losing control and being vulnerable. Our relationship taught me the importance of opening up and communicating my feelings, even when it feels uncomfortable."

Testimony of Rachel, 32 years old:

"I've always been fiercely independent and focused on my career. When I met Michael, he was understanding and supportive of my ambitions. We had fun together and enjoyed each other's company, but I struggled to let him into my emotional world. Michael wanted a deeper connection, but I kept him at arm's length, afraid of losing my sense of self. It took me a while to realize that emotional detachment was my way of protecting my independence. Our relationship taught me that while I value companionship, I need to find someone who respects my need for space and understands my boundaries."

Testimony of Jason, 36 years old:

"I grew up in a family where emotions were seen as a weakness. When I met Sarah, I was drawn to her kindness and compassion. We had a great connection and shared many interests, but I struggled to express my emotions openly. Sarah wanted emotional intimacy, but I found it difficult to let my guard down. I feared being judged or misunderstood. Our relationship taught me that emotional detachment wasn't serving me well. It was only through therapy and self-reflection that I started to understand the roots of my emotional barriers and work towards building healthier emotional connections."

Testimony of Megan, 25 years old:

"I've always been a private person and find it hard to share my deepest thoughts and feelings. When I met Adam, he was caring and attentive. We enjoyed each other's company and had fun together, but I struggled to open up emotionally. Adam wanted to know more about me, but I kept conversations light and surface-level. It wasn't that I didn't care for him—I did—but I found it hard to break down my emotional walls. Our relationship taught me the importance of vulnerability and how it's okay to share my true self with someone I trust."

Testimony of David, 31 years old:

"I've always valued my personal space and independence. When I met Jessica, she was understanding and supportive of my need for freedom. We had a good connection and enjoyed spending time together, but I struggled with emotional intimacy. Jessica wanted a deeper emotional connection, but I found it hard to reciprocate. I enjoyed our time together but felt suffocated when emotions became too intense. Our relationship taught me that while I cherish companionship, I need to find a balance that respects my boundaries and allows me to maintain my sense of self."

These testimonies provide a variety of perspectives on emotional detachment in relationships, illustrating how individuals navigate their emotional barriers, personal growth, and the complexities of forming meaningful connections.

Chapter 4: Lack of Attachment to Traditional Relationship Norms

In today's evolving landscape of relationships, many individuals and couples are exploring dynamics that deviate from traditional norms. One such dynamic is cuckolding, which can be appealing to those who are not strongly attached to conventional ideas of monogamy and exclusivity. Here's why some men might find fulfillment in this arrangement due to a lack of attachment to traditional relationship norms:

1. Embracing Sexual Exploration

For men who are open-minded and curious about their sexuality, cuckolding offers a way to explore new territories. They are often not confined by the conventional boundaries of monogamy, seeing value in experiences that involve multiple partners. This openness allows them to delve into fantasies that might be considered taboo or unconventional.

2. Redefining Intimacy and Trust

Traditional relationships often equate exclusivity with trust and intimacy. However, men who embrace cuckolding may view these concepts differently. For them, intimacy and trust are built through transparency, communication, and the freedom to explore desires without judgment. By allowing their partner to engage with someone else, they feel a unique form of trust and connection that transcends traditional norms.

3. Challenging Societal Expectations

Society places significant pressure on individuals to conform to standard relationship models. Men who participate in cuckolding often challenge these societal expectations, seeking a path that aligns more closely with their personal beliefs and desires. This rebellion against conventional norms can be empowering, allowing them to live authentically.

4. Emphasizing Mutual Pleasure

In non-traditional relationships, mutual pleasure and satisfaction are often prioritized over adherence to social norms. Men who agree to cuckolding may do so because they derive pleasure from their partner's pleasure. The idea that their partner's happiness and sexual fulfillment are paramount can be more important than sticking to traditional notions of fidelity.

5. Experiencing Novel Emotional Dynamics

Cuckolding introduces a range of emotions that are less common in traditional relationships, such as jealousy, compersion, and arousal from voyeurism. Men who lack attachment to traditional norms may find these emotional dynamics intriguing and fulfilling. The complexity of these feelings can add depth and excitement to their relationship.

6. Flexibility and Fluidity in Relationships

Traditional relationships often come with rigid roles and expectations. Men who are less attached to these norms may prefer the flexibility and fluidity that cuckolding offers. This dynamic allows them to redefine their roles within the relationship, creating a more personalized and adaptive partnership that suits their unique needs and desires.

7. Encouraging Open Communication

Non-traditional relationships, including those involving cuckolding, require a high level of open and honest communication. Men who thrive in these dynamics are typically comfortable discussing their deepest desires, fears, and boundaries. This open dialogue can strengthen the relationship, fostering a deeper understanding and connection between partners.

8. Celebrating Individual Autonomy

In traditional relationships, autonomy can sometimes be sacrificed for the sake of unity and exclusivity. Men who engage in cuckolding often celebrate individual autonomy, recognizing that each partner has unique desires and needs. By supporting their partner's freedom to explore, they reinforce their commitment to each other's personal growth and happiness.

Conclusion

The lack of attachment to traditional relationship norms can lead some men to find fulfillment in cuckolding dynamics. By embracing sexual exploration, redefining intimacy and trust, challenging societal expectations, emphasizing mutual pleasure, experiencing novel emotional dynamics, valuing flexibility and fluidity, encouraging open communication, and celebrating individual autonomy, they create a relationship that is uniquely tailored to their desires and values. This approach fosters a deeper connection and mutual satisfaction, allowing both partners to thrive in a non-traditional but deeply meaningful relationship.

Alternative Relationship Values

Some individuals and couples may reject or feel less bound by traditional relationship norms and expectations, including monogamy. This perspective can be a significant factor in why some men find fulfillment in cuckolding dynamics. Here's a deeper look into how alternative relationship values influence their choices:

1. Redefining Relationship Boundaries

Couples who embrace alternative relationship values often redefine the boundaries of their relationship. For them, love and commitment are not necessarily tied to sexual exclusivity. By exploring cuckolding, they create a unique set of rules and understandings that cater to their individual needs and desires.

2. Emphasizing Personal Freedom

In relationships that prioritize personal freedom, partners are encouraged to explore their own desires and fantasies. Men who are part of such relationships might agree to cuckolding because it allows both partners to experience greater freedom. This dynamic supports the idea that one's sexual and emotional fulfillment can be pursued without conventional restrictions.

3. Prioritizing Communication and Consent

Alternative relationship values often place a strong emphasis on communication and consent. Men who participate in cuckolding typically engage in extensive discussions with their partners about boundaries, desires, and feelings. This open communication ensures that both partners are comfortable and consensual in their exploration, strengthening their bond.

4. Celebrating Diversity in Desire

Couples with alternative relationship values celebrate the diversity of human desire. They understand that attraction and fantasies can vary widely and do not fit neatly into traditional relationship models. Cuckolding can be a way to honor and explore these diverse desires in a consensual and supportive environment.

5. Building Trust Through Transparency

Trust is crucial in any relationship, and for those with alternative values, it is built through transparency and honesty. Men who engage in cuckolding with their partners often find that this level of openness about desires and fantasies enhances their trust. Knowing that their partner is willing to share and explore these desires openly can be deeply reassuring.

6. Exploring Power Dynamics

Alternative relationships can provide a safe space to explore power dynamics that might be taboo in traditional settings. Cuckolding allows men to experience and play with different roles, such as submission, dominance, or voyeurism. This exploration can lead to a richer understanding of their own and their partner's sexuality.

7. Enhancing Emotional and Sexual Satisfaction

By rejecting conventional norms, couples can focus more on what genuinely enhances their emotional and sexual satisfaction. Cuckolding might bring new levels of excitement and fulfillment that traditional monogamy does not offer. This focus on personal satisfaction over societal expectations can strengthen the relationship.

8. Practicing Compersion

Compersion, the joy one feels from their partner's happiness, is often a core value in alternative relationships. Men who agree to cuckolding may do so because they find joy and satisfaction in seeing their partner pleasured by someone else. This compersion can foster a deeper emotional connection and mutual respect.

Conclusion

Alternative relationship values encourage couples to move beyond traditional norms and create dynamics that are uniquely satisfying for them. For some men, agreeing to cuckolding is a way to embrace personal freedom, redefine relationship boundaries, enhance communication and consent, celebrate diverse desires, build trust through transparency, explore power dynamics, and practice compersion. By focusing on what brings genuine fulfillment rather than adhering to conventional expectations, these couples can cultivate a relationship that is deeply enriching and authentic.

Freedom and Autonomy

Many individuals and couples place a high value on personal freedom and autonomy in their relationships, including sexual autonomy for their partner. This perspective can significantly influence why some men find fulfillment in cuckolding dynamics. Here's a deeper look into how prioritizing freedom and autonomy shapes their choices:

1. Respect for Individual Desires

In relationships that prioritize freedom and autonomy, both partners respect each other's individual desires and fantasies. Men who agree to cuckolding often do so because they want to honor their partner's sexual autonomy and provide them the freedom to explore their own desires. This mutual respect enhances the trust and bond between partners.

2. Emphasizing Mutual Consent

A relationship built on autonomy emphasizes mutual consent and open communication. Men who participate in cuckolding typically ensure that all actions are consensual and that both partners feel comfortable with the arrangement. This focus on consent reinforces the idea that both partners are equally respected and valued in their relationship.

3. Encouraging Exploration

Freedom and autonomy in relationships encourage exploration and experimentation. Men who are open to cuckolding often appreciate the opportunity to explore their own boundaries and fantasies in a safe and consensual manner. This exploration can lead to personal growth and a deeper understanding of their own and their partner's sexuality.

4. Supporting Personal Growth

Couples who prioritize autonomy support each other's personal growth and fulfillment. For some men, allowing their partner to engage with someone else sexually can be a way to support their partner's sexual freedom and happiness. This support is seen as a positive contribution to the overall health and satisfaction of the relationship.

5. Reducing Feelings of Ownership

Traditional relationships often come with a sense of ownership over a partner's body and sexuality. In contrast, relationships that value autonomy reject this notion, viewing each partner as an independent individual. Men who agree to cuckolding do so because they reject the idea of possessing their partner, instead embracing their partner's right to sexual freedom.

6. Enhancing Emotional Intimacy

By prioritizing autonomy, couples often enhance their emotional intimacy. Open discussions about desires and boundaries can lead to a deeper emotional connection. Men who support their partner's sexual autonomy find that this openness and honesty strengthen their relationship, creating a more profound and trusting bond.

7. Balancing Independence and Togetherness

Freedom and autonomy in relationships allow for a healthy balance between independence and togetherness. Men who engage in cuckolding often do so to ensure that both partners maintain their individuality while also sharing a deep and connected relationship. This balance prevents feelings of suffocation and promotes a more harmonious partnership.

8. Promoting Equality

Relationships that emphasize autonomy promote equality between partners. Men who agree to cuckolding do so from a place of equality, understanding that both partners have the right to pursue their own desires. This approach fosters a sense of partnership and mutual respect, where each individual's needs and wants are valued equally.

Conclusion

Prioritizing freedom and autonomy in relationships allows couples to move beyond traditional norms and create dynamics that honor each partner's individuality and desires. For some men, agreeing to cuckolding is a way to respect their partner's sexual autonomy, emphasize mutual consent, encourage exploration, support personal growth, reduce feelings of ownership, enhance emotional intimacy, balance independence and togetherness, and promote equality. By focusing on these values, couples can cultivate a relationship that is deeply fulfilling, respectful, and supportive of both partners' needs and aspirations.

Chapter 5: Communication and Trust Dynamics

Effective communication and trust are cornerstones of any successful relationship, and they become even more crucial in non-traditional dynamics like cuckolding. Here's an in-depth exploration of how communication and trust dynamics play a pivotal role in these relationships:

1. Establishing Clear Boundaries

Communication is essential for setting and understanding boundaries in a cuckolding dynamic. Both partners need to openly discuss their limits, expectations, and comfort levels. Men who agree to cuckolding often do so after thorough conversations that establish what is acceptable and what is not, ensuring that both partners feel safe and respected.

2. Regular Check-Ins

Regular check-ins help maintain trust and ensure that both partners are comfortable with the arrangement. These conversations allow them to express any concerns, fears, or desires that may arise. Men who engage in cuckolding find that these frequent discussions reinforce their bond and prevent misunderstandings.

3. Honesty and Transparency

Honesty and transparency are vital in building and maintaining trust. Men who participate in cuckolding must be honest about their feelings and reactions to the situation. Similarly, their partners need to be transparent about their experiences and interactions with others. This openness ensures that both partners remain on the same page and fosters a deeper level of trust.

4. Handling Jealousy

Jealousy is a natural emotion that can arise in cuckolding dynamics. Effective communication allows partners to address and manage these feelings constructively. Men who agree to cuckolding often find that talking openly about their jealousy helps to mitigate its impact and strengthens their emotional resilience.

5. Mutual Reassurance

Providing and seeking reassurance is crucial for maintaining trust. Men who are involved in cuckolding dynamics often need reassurance from their partners that their primary relationship remains strong and valued. This mutual reassurance helps to reinforce the commitment and emotional connection between partners.

6. Emotional Support

Cuckolding dynamics require a high level of emotional support from both partners. Men who engage in these relationships often rely on their partners for emotional validation and support, especially when navigating complex feelings. Open communication ensures that both partners feel supported and understood.

7. Affirming the Primary Relationship

Affirming the importance of the primary relationship is key to maintaining trust. Men who participate in cuckolding dynamics often reaffirm their love and commitment to their primary partner, ensuring that the relationship remains the central focus. This affirmation helps to build a strong foundation of trust and security.

8. Flexibility and Adaptability

Effective communication allows couples to be flexible and adapt to changing circumstances. Men who engage in cuckolding often find that their needs and boundaries may evolve over time. Regular discussions and a willingness to adapt help to ensure that the relationship remains healthy and fulfilling.

9. Building Emotional Intimacy

Open and honest communication fosters emotional intimacy. Men who agree to cuckolding often experience a deeper emotional connection with their partner as they navigate their desires and boundaries together. This increased intimacy strengthens their overall relationship.

10. Conflict Resolution

Conflicts and disagreements are inevitable in any relationship, and cuckolding dynamics are no exception. Effective communication skills are essential for resolving conflicts constructively. Men who participate in cuckolding find that being able to talk through issues calmly and respectfully helps to maintain trust and harmony in the relationship.

Conclusion

Communication and trust dynamics are crucial in cuckolding relationships. By establishing clear boundaries, conducting regular check-ins, practicing honesty and transparency, handling jealousy constructively, providing mutual reassurance, offering emotional support, affirming the primary relationship, maintaining flexibility, building emotional intimacy, and resolving conflicts effectively, couples can navigate these complex dynamics successfully. Through open communication and strong trust, they can create a deeply fulfilling and resilient relationship that honors both partners' needs and desires.

Embracing Openness: Emily's Journey into Love, Trust, and Personal Growth

In a world where traditional relationship norms are increasingly challenged, Emily's journey into an open relationship with her partner, Tom, offers a compelling perspective on love, trust, and personal growth. Her testimonial provides a glimpse into the reasons why she believes exploring relationships with other men has not only deepened her connection with Tom but also enhanced their overall relationship dynamics. Through candid conversations and a commitment to honesty, Emily shares how their decision has transformed their relationship, challenging conventional ideas and fostering a deeper sense of emotional fulfillment. Here, Emily narrates her story of navigating love, trust, and the freedom to explore, offering insights that challenge and inspire.

My name is Emily, and I have been in a deeply fulfilling open relationship with my partner, Tom, for the past three years. When I first broached the idea of exploring relationships with other men, it was not without careful consideration and many heart-to-heart conversations with Tom. I wanted to ensure that this was something we both genuinely wanted and that it would benefit our relationship rather than harm it. What I found was that having the freedom to engage with other men has had a profoundly positive impact on both Tom and our relationship as a whole. First and foremost, it has forced us to communicate more openly and honestly than ever before.

Discussing our desires, boundaries, and feelings has built a level of trust that I never imagined possible. Tom knows he can express his concerns and desires without fear of judgment, and I feel the same way. This transparency has brought us closer, making our emotional bond stronger than ever. Additionally, allowing myself the freedom to explore other relationships has made me more confident and self-assured, which in turn has positively influenced how I interact with Tom.

I am happier and more fulfilled, and this joy naturally spills over into our relationship. Tom has shared that seeing me happy and fulfilled makes him happy too, and it takes the pressure off him to be the sole provider of my sexual and emotional needs. Interestingly, our own sexual relationship has become more vibrant and exciting. The variety and new experiences I encounter enhance my sexual satisfaction, which benefits Tom as well because we can share and explore these new dynamics together.

On a deeper level, this arrangement has allowed Tom to confront and work through feelings of jealousy and insecurity, which has made him more confident and self-assured. Knowing that our relationship is strong enough to withstand and even thrive in this unconventional setup has been empowering for both of us. It has reaffirmed our commitment to each other and solidified the trust that forms the foundation of our partnership. By stepping away from traditional relationship norms, we have crafted a unique dynamic that truly resonates with us and brings us both immense satisfaction. Tom's ability to find joy in my happiness, even when it involves other men, has deepened our emotional connection and strengthened our bond. In this way, our open relationship has not only brought us closer but also allowed us to grow individually and as a couple, making our relationship richer and more fulfilling than ever before.

Embracing Love Beyond Boundaries: A Journey into Non-Monogamy

In the realm of modern relationships, traditional boundaries are increasingly being challenged as couples explore new dynamics to nurture deeper connections and personal growth. This story delves into the journey of James and Sarah, a couple whose love defies conventional norms. When Sarah proposed exploring relationships with other men, James found himself confronted with new perspectives on love, trust, and commitment. Their journey into non-monogamy became a transformative experience, redefining their relationship on a foundation of openness, communication, and mutual support. Through their story, we explore the complexities of modern love and the profound ways in which couples navigate the uncharted territories of fidelity and personal fulfillment.

My name is James, and I'm 35 years old. My partner, Sarah, and I have been together for over a decade. About three years ago, Sarah approached me with the idea of exploring relationships with other men. At first, I admit I was taken aback. Like many people, I had grown up with the belief that monogamy was the only way to show commitment. However, Sarah's perspective challenged me to reconsider what it truly means to support someone you love.

Sarah is a vibrant and adventurous woman, always passionate about exploring new experiences and understanding different aspects of herself. She explained that for her, having the freedom to connect with others romantically and sexually didn't diminish her love for me; instead, it enriched her life and brought a deeper level of fulfillment. Hearing her perspective was eye-opening. It made me realize that our relationship could evolve beyond traditional boundaries while still maintaining its core values of love, respect, and support.

Since then, our journey into non-monogamy has been one of mutual exploration and growth. It's not about seeking excitement or novelty but about nurturing our individual identities within the context of a loving partnership. We communicate openly about our feelings, fears, and desires, which has deepened our emotional intimacy in ways I hadn't imagined. Through this process, I've learned to confront my own insecurities and trust in Sarah's commitment to our relationship.

Allowing Sarah the freedom to explore has taught me valuable lessons about love and partnership. It's shown me that true love isn't about possession but about celebrating each other's autonomy and happiness. Our relationship isn't conventional, but it's uniquely ours, built on a foundation of trust, respect, and a shared commitment to personal growth. Embracing this journey with Sarah has enriched my life immeasurably, and I wouldn't trade it for anything.

Understanding High Trust Levels in Relationships

High trust levels in relationships refer to a deep sense of confidence and security that partners have in each other's intentions, actions, and commitments. This level of trust is often built over time through consistent communication, honesty, reliability, and mutual respect. In rare cases, exceptionally strong trust and communication within the relationship might lead individuals, including men, to feel secure even when faced with the possibility or reality of infidelity.

Factors Contributing to High Trust Levels:

1. **Open Communication:** Partners in relationships with high trust levels communicate openly and honestly about their feelings, desires, and boundaries. They discuss difficult topics, including potential challenges or temptations, without fear of judgment or reprisal.
2. **Shared Values and Commitments:** Couples with high trust levels often share core values and long-term commitments to each other's well-being and happiness. They prioritize the emotional connection and mutual

support over individual desires or external temptations.

3. **Past Experiences:** Positive experiences and successful resolutions of challenges in the past contribute to building trust. Partners may have overcome previous difficulties together, reinforcing their belief in each other's loyalty and commitment.

4. **Mutual Respect and Empathy:** Respectful and empathetic behavior towards each other fosters trust. Partners actively listen to each other's concerns, validate their emotions, and work together to address any issues that arise in the relationship.

Impact on Attitudes Towards Infidelity:

● **Feelings of Security:** In relationships with high trust levels, individuals may feel secure in the belief that their partner's actions are guided by mutual respect and commitment. They may interpret potential instances of infidelity as isolated incidents or misunderstandings rather than a betrayal of trust.

● **Forgiveness and Understanding:** Partners with high trust levels are more likely to approach conflicts or challenges, such as infidelity, with forgiveness and understanding. They may empathize with each other's vulnerabilities and work towards reconciliation and rebuilding trust rather than immediately resorting to judgment or blame.

● **Resilience in Adversity:** Couples with high trust levels often exhibit resilience in the face of adversity. They may view challenges, including infidelity, as opportunities to strengthen their bond through honest communication, mutual support, and renewed commitments to each other.

Challenges and Considerations:

● **Maintaining Trust:** Building and maintaining high trust levels requires ongoing effort and commitment from both partners. It involves consistent communication, transparency, and a willingness to address issues promptly and constructively.

● **Individual Differences:** Trust levels can vary between individuals and relationships. Factors such as personality traits, past experiences, and cultural beliefs may influence how trust is established and maintained within a partnership.

● **Boundaries and Expectations:** Even in relationships with high trust levels, it's essential for partners to discuss and respect each other's boundaries and expectations regarding fidelity and emotional exclusivity. Clear communication helps prevent misunderstandings and promotes mutual understanding.

In summary, high trust levels in relationships can create a foundation of security and understanding that may mitigate feelings of insecurity or distress in the face of infidelity. Trust, built on open communication, shared values, and mutual respect, plays a crucial role in how individuals perceive and respond to challenges within their relationships.

Exploring Mutual Understanding in Relationships

Mutual understanding in relationships refers to a shared agreement or arrangement between partners regarding various aspects of their relationship, including fidelity and boundaries. This understanding allows couples to establish unconventional boundaries that may deviate from traditional norms but are agreed upon by both parties.

Factors Contributing to Mutual Understanding:

1. **Open Communication:** Effective communication is key to establishing mutual understanding in relationships. Partners openly discuss their expectations, desires, and boundaries regarding fidelity, allowing for a clear understanding of each other's perspectives.
2. **Respect for Individuality:** Couples with mutual understanding respect each other's individuality and autonomy. They acknowledge that each person may have unique needs or desires regarding relationships and work together to find solutions that accommodate both parties.
3. **Shared Values and Goals:** Partners often share core values and long-term goals, which guide their decisions and agreements regarding fidelity. They prioritize their emotional connection and mutual well-being while remaining open to exploring unconventional relationship dynamics.
4. **Negotiation and Compromise:** Establishing unconventional boundaries requires negotiation and compromise from both partners. They may discuss and adjust their boundaries over time based on their evolving needs, experiences, and mutual agreement.

Impact on Relationship Dynamics:

● **Increased Trust and Security:** Mutual understanding fosters a sense of trust and security within the relationship. Partners feel confident that their agreements regarding fidelity are respected and honored, reducing potential feelings of jealousy or insecurity.

● **Flexibility and Adaptability:** Couples with mutual understanding often exhibit flexibility and adaptability in navigating challenges, including issues related to fidelity. They may redefine their boundaries or agreements as their relationship evolves, ensuring ongoing mutual satisfaction and fulfillment.

● **Emotional Intimacy:** By openly discussing and negotiating their boundaries, partners in relationships with mutual understanding deepen their emotional intimacy. They feel understood and supported in their individual needs and desires, fostering a stronger bond and connection.

Challenges and Considerations:

● **External Perceptions:** Unconventional boundaries regarding fidelity may be misunderstood or judged by others. Partners in such relationships may need to navigate societal expectations and stigma while maintaining confidence in their mutual agreements.

● **Consistency and Honesty:** Maintaining mutual understanding requires consistent honesty and transparency from both partners. They must communicate openly about their feelings, experiences, and any changes in their boundaries to ensure mutual respect and trust.

● **Personal Growth:** Individuals in relationships with unconventional boundaries may experience personal growth and self-discovery as they navigate their unique dynamics. They learn to prioritize their emotional well-being while respecting their partner's needs and boundaries.

In summary, mutual understanding in relationships allows couples to establish unconventional boundaries regarding fidelity based on open communication, respect for individuality, and shared agreements. This approach fosters trust, security, and emotional intimacy, enabling partners to navigate challenges and complexities while maintaining mutual satisfaction and fulfillment.

Testimony

In the realm of modern relationships, the concept of fidelity and its boundaries is often open to interpretation. For many couples, traditional notions of exclusivity may not fully capture the depth and nuances of their partnerships. Instead, they navigate their commitment through mutual understanding—a shared agreement that prioritizes emotional connection, respect for individual autonomy, and personal growth.

The following testimonies from various couples illustrate how mutual understanding shapes their relationships. Each couple has chosen to redefine fidelity based on their unique values and dynamics, fostering bonds that are strengthened by honesty, empathy, and a deep respect for each other's journey. These testimonies highlight the diverse ways in which couples navigate love, trust, and commitment in today's ever-evolving landscape of relationships.

Testimony of James and Sarah:

"In our relationship, James and I prioritize mutual understanding and respect. We've agreed to a non-traditional approach to fidelity, focusing on emotional connection and individual growth. This agreement has strengthened our bond and allowed us to support each other's personal journeys."

Testimony of Michael and Emily:

"Mutual understanding in our relationship means honoring each other's autonomy and emotional needs. Michael and I have redefined fidelity based on our shared values of honesty and communication. This approach has fostered a partnership where we both feel valued and supported."

Testimony of David and Rachel:

"For David and me, mutual understanding involves open communication and empathy. We've embraced a flexible approach to fidelity, prioritizing trust and personal growth. This understanding has created a foundation of respect and resilience in our relationship."

Testimony of Daniel and Jessica:

"Daniel and I have built our relationship on mutual understanding and mutual respect. We prioritize emotional intimacy and honesty, allowing us to navigate challenges with compassion. This approach has deepened our connection and strengthened our commitment to each other."

Testimony of Matthew and Olivia:

"Matthew and I value mutual understanding in our relationship. We've chosen to redefine fidelity based on our shared values and commitment to personal growth. This has allowed us to build a supportive partnership where we both feel understood and valued."

Testimony of Andrew and Megan:

"In our relationship, Andrew and I emphasize mutual understanding and support. We've agreed on the importance of communication and respect for each other's boundaries. This has fostered a relationship where we can grow together while honoring our individuality."

Testimony of Ryan and Nicole:

"Ryan and I prioritize mutual understanding in our relationship. We've embraced a non-traditional view of fidelity that values emotional connection and empathy. This understanding has created a strong foundation of trust and love between us."

Testimony of Eric and Samantha:

"Eric and I have established our relationship on mutual understanding and shared values. We've redefined fidelity to include open communication and personal growth. This approach has allowed us to build a partnership that is supportive and fulfilling."

Testimony of Jason and Lauren:

"Jason and I value mutual understanding in our relationship. We've chosen to prioritize emotional intimacy and respect for each other's individuality. This has created a relationship where we can navigate challenges with honesty and empathy."

Testimony of Adam and Emily:

"For Adam and me, mutual understanding means respecting each other's autonomy and emotional needs. We've agreed on a flexible approach to fidelity, focusing on trust and communication. This understanding has strengthened our bond and allowed us to grow together."

Chapter 6 : Personal or Psychological Factors in Relationships

In navigating relationships, various personal and psychological factors play crucial roles in shaping dynamics and outcomes. These factors encompass individual characteristics, past experiences, and internal processes that influence how individuals perceive, engage in, and sustain relationships.

1. **Attachment Styles**: The attachment theory posits that early childhood experiences with caregivers shape individuals' attachment styles in adulthood. Secure attachment fosters trust, intimacy, and comfort in relationships, while insecure attachment may manifest as anxious or avoidant behaviors, affecting relationship dynamics.
2. **Personality Traits**: Personalities vary widely, impacting how individuals communicate, handle conflict, and express affection in relationships. Traits like openness, agreeableness, conscientiousness, and emotional stability can shape compatibility and interaction patterns between partners.
3. **Communication Skills**: Effective communication is fundamental to healthy relationships. The ability to express needs, listen actively, and resolve conflicts constructively promotes understanding and strengthens emotional bonds.
4. **Emotional Intelligence**: Emotional intelligence involves the awareness, management, and expression of emotions. Partners with high emotional intelligence can navigate complex feelings, empathize with each other's experiences, and maintain emotional intimacy.
5. **Past Experiences**: Previous relationships, family dynamics, and life experiences influence individuals' expectations, fears, and behaviors in current relationships. Unresolved past traumas or negative experiences may impact trust, vulnerability, and commitment levels.
6. **Values and Beliefs**: Shared values, beliefs, and goals provide a foundation for relationship compatibility and mutual understanding. Differences in religious beliefs, cultural backgrounds, or life priorities can pose challenges but also offer opportunities for growth and compromise.
7. **Self-Esteem and Self-Worth**: Individuals with healthy self-esteem tend to have more fulfilling relationships, as they can assert boundaries, receive love, and support their partners without relying solely on external validation.
8. **Stress and Coping Mechanisms**: External stressors such as work pressure, financial challenges, or health issues can affect relationship quality. Effective coping mechanisms, such as problem-solving skills and emotional support from partners, contribute to resilience and relationship satisfaction.
9. **Commitment and Attachment**: The degree of commitment and attachment partners feel toward each other influences relationship longevity and emotional investment. Commitment involves dedication to mutual growth, shared goals, and navigating challenges together.
10. **Personal Growth and Development**: Relationships offer opportunities for personal growth and development. Partners who encourage each other's aspirations, celebrate achievements, and navigate setbacks collaboratively foster a supportive environment for individual flourishing within the relationship.

Understanding these personal and psychological factors can help individuals and couples cultivate healthier, more fulfilling relationships by fostering self-awareness, empathy, and effective communication.

Origins of Attachment Theory

Attachment theory, initially proposed by John Bowlby in the 1950s, emphasizes the importance of early caregiving experiences in shaping individuals' emotional development and interpersonal relationships throughout life. Bowlby observed that infants form attachments to their primary caregivers as a means of seeking security, comfort, and protection. These early attachments lay the foundation for internal working models—mental representations of relationships—that influence how individuals perceive themselves, others, and their interactions.

Types of Attachment Styles

1. Secure Attachment:

○ **Description**: Developed in response to consistently responsive caregiving, secure attachment is characterized by trust, emotional openness, and comfort with intimacy.

○ **Behavioral Traits**: Adults with secure attachment styles tend to feel confident in themselves and their relationships. They are comfortable expressing emotions, seeking support, and establishing healthy boundaries.

2. Insecure Attachment:

○ **Anxious-Preoccupied Attachment**:

▪ **Description**: Individuals with this style may have experienced inconsistent caregiving—sometimes responsive, sometimes neglectful—which leads to anxiety about relationships.

▪ **Behavioral Traits**: They often seek reassurance, fear rejection or abandonment, and may exhibit clingy or demanding behaviors in relationships.

○ **Dismissive-Avoidant Attachment**:

▪ **Description**: Resulting from caregivers who were dismissive or emotionally unavailable, this style is marked by a reluctance to rely on others and a tendency to suppress emotions.

▪ **Behavioral Traits**: People with dismissive-avoidant attachment styles value independence, may avoid intimacy, and prioritize self-reliance over emotional connection.

○ **Fearful-Avoidant Attachment**:

▪ **Description**: Stemming from caregivers who were both intrusive and rejecting, this style combines aspects of anxiety and avoidance.

▪ **Behavioral Traits**: Individuals may desire closeness but fear vulnerability or rejection, leading to conflicted behaviors in relationships—seeking intimacy while pushing others away.

Impact on Relationships

- **Communication and Conflict**: Attachment styles significantly influence how individuals communicate and manage conflicts in relationships. Securely attached individuals tend to communicate openly and resolve conflicts constructively, whereas insecure attachment styles can lead to misunderstandings, emotional volatility, or avoidance during conflicts.

- **Intimacy and Trust**: Secure attachment fosters a sense of emotional safety and trust, allowing for deeper intimacy and mutual support. In contrast, insecure attachment may hinder the development of trust and intimacy, as anxieties about rejection or abandonment can undermine relationship closeness.

- **Relationship Dynamics**: Attachment styles influence partner selection, relationship satisfaction, and longevity. Individuals with secure attachment styles are more likely to form stable, fulfilling relationships, while insecure attachment may contribute to patterns of instability, dissatisfaction, or repeated relational difficulties.

Developmental and Therapeutic Considerations

- **Early Childhood Influences**: Attachment styles are primarily shaped by early interactions with caregivers. Consistent responsiveness, emotional attunement, and nurturing support promote secure attachment, while inconsistent or inadequate caregiving can contribute to insecure attachment patterns.

- **Therapeutic Interventions**: Understanding attachment styles is crucial in therapeutic settings, where interventions aim to promote secure attachment and address the impact of early relational experiences. Therapies such as Attachment-Based Therapy (ABT) or Emotionally Focused Therapy (EFT) focus on healing attachment wounds, improving communication skills, and fostering secure relational patterns.

- **Personal Growth**: Awareness of one's attachment style can facilitate personal growth by identifying relational patterns, enhancing self-awareness, and developing more secure attachment behaviors. Individuals can cultivate healthier relationships by challenging insecure attachment patterns, exploring vulnerability, and seeking supportive connections.

In conclusion, attachment theory offers valuable insights into the complexities of human relationships, highlighting the profound impact of early caregiving experiences on emotional development and relational dynamics throughout life. By understanding and addressing attachment styles, individuals can nurture more secure, satisfying relationships and embark on a path of personal growth and healing.

Personality Traits and Their Impact on Relationships

Personality traits play a significant role in shaping how individuals perceive, engage in, and navigate relationships. Here's a breakdown of key personality traits and their implications:

1. **Openness to Experience**:

   ○ **Description**: Reflects curiosity, creativity, and openness to new ideas and experiences.

○ **Impact on Relationships**: Partners high in openness may seek novelty and intellectual stimulation in relationships. They may value exploration and growth, enjoying shared interests and diverse experiences with their partner.

2. **Conscientiousness**:

○ **Description**: Indicates organization, responsibility, and self-discipline.

○ **Impact on Relationships**: Conscientious individuals are reliable and goal-oriented in relationships. They prioritize commitment, follow through on promises, and maintain orderly and structured interactions.

3. **Extraversion**:

○ **Description**: Characterized by sociability, assertiveness, and enjoyment of social interactions.

○ **Impact on Relationships**: Extraverts thrive in social settings and seek connection and engagement with others, including their partner. They often enjoy shared activities, social gatherings, and lively conversations.

4. **Agreeableness**:

○ **Description**: Reflects kindness, empathy, and cooperation.

○ **Impact on Relationships**: Individuals high in agreeableness prioritize harmony and mutual understanding in relationships. They are compassionate, considerate of their partner's feelings, and adept at resolving conflicts diplomatically.

5. **Emotional Stability (Neuroticism)**:

○ **Description**: Refers to emotional resilience, calmness, and stability under stress.

○ **Impact on Relationships**: High emotional stability promotes emotional balance and resilience in relationships. Individuals are less likely to react impulsively or escalate conflicts, fostering a secure and supportive relational environment.

Compatibility and Interaction Patterns

● **Complementary Traits**: Partners with complementary personality traits may balance each other's strengths and weaknesses. For example, a conscientious person may benefit from the spontaneity of a partner high in openness.

● **Conflict Resolution**: Personality traits influence how individuals approach and resolve conflicts. For instance, individuals high in agreeableness may prioritize compromise and seek win-win solutions, whereas those low in agreeableness may struggle with negotiation and compromise.

● **Communication Styles**: Personality traits shape communication styles, affecting how partners express emotions, articulate needs, and interpret each other's behaviors. Open communication and understanding of each other's personality traits can enhance relational satisfaction and intimacy.

Practical Implications and Relationship Dynamics

- **Self-Awareness and Growth**: Awareness of one's own personality traits and those of their partner promotes self-reflection, empathy, and mutual understanding. Couples can leverage their strengths and navigate challenges more effectively by acknowledging and respecting differences in personality.

- **Long-Term Dynamics**: Personality traits contribute to long-term relationship satisfaction and stability. Couples who align in core personality traits and adapt positively to differences may experience greater resilience and longevity in their relationship.

Understanding the influence of personality traits on relationships enhances relational dynamics, promotes mutual growth, and fosters a deeper connection between partners. By recognizing and valuing each other's unique traits, individuals can cultivate fulfilling, supportive, and resilient relationships over time.

Communication Skills in Relationships

Effective communication is essential for fostering understanding, resolving conflicts, and building strong emotional connections between partners. Here's a deeper dive into the key aspects of communication skills:

1. **Expressing Needs and Emotions**:

o **Description**: Clear and assertive communication allows individuals to express their thoughts, feelings, and needs openly and honestly.

o **Impact on Relationships**: Partners who effectively express themselves create an atmosphere of trust and mutual respect. They feel heard and understood, which strengthens emotional intimacy and promotes healthy relationship dynamics.

2. **Active Listening**:

o **Description**: Active listening involves fully concentrating on what the other person is saying, understanding their perspective, and responding thoughtfully.

o **Impact on Relationships**: Active listening promotes empathy and validation. It shows respect for the partner's feelings and perspectives, fostering a supportive environment where both individuals feel valued and understood.

3. **Nonverbal Communication**:

o **Description**: Nonverbal cues such as body language, facial expressions, and gestures convey emotions and intentions.

o **Impact on Relationships**: Being attentive to nonverbal cues enhances understanding and empathy in communication. Partners can better interpret each other's feelings and reactions, even when words are unsaid.

4. **Conflict Resolution Skills**:

○ **Description**: Constructive conflict resolution involves addressing disagreements calmly, listening to each other's viewpoints, and seeking mutually beneficial solutions.

○ **Impact on Relationships**: Effective conflict resolution strengthens the relationship by reducing misunderstandings and resentment. It promotes compromise, respect for differing opinions, and collaborative problem-solving.

Practical Applications

● **Assertiveness**: Assertive communication empowers individuals to express themselves confidently while respecting others' perspectives and boundaries.

● **Clarity and Consistency**: Clear and consistent communication helps prevent misunderstandings and promotes alignment in goals, expectations, and decision-making.

● **Emotional Regulation**: Managing emotions during communication enhances the ability to respond calmly and empathetically, even in challenging situations.

Building Strong Emotional Bonds

● **Trust and Intimacy**: Effective communication builds trust by promoting transparency and authenticity. Partners who communicate openly and honestly develop deeper emotional bonds and a sense of security in the relationship.

● **Shared Understanding**: Clear communication fosters a shared understanding of each other's values, needs, and aspirations. This mutual understanding strengthens emotional connection and promotes mutual support.

Continuous Improvement

● **Skills Development**: Developing communication skills is an ongoing process that requires practice, feedback, and willingness to learn from each other.

● **Couples Therapy**: Couples may benefit from therapy to enhance communication skills, resolve persistent issues, and strengthen their relationship foundation.

Effective communication skills are foundational to maintaining healthy, fulfilling relationships. By prioritizing clear expression, active listening, and constructive conflict resolution, couples can cultivate deeper understanding, trust, and emotional intimacy in their relationship journey.

Emotional Intelligence in Relationships

Emotional intelligence refers to the ability to recognize, understand, manage, and express emotions effectively. In the context of relationships, individuals with high emotional intelligence demonstrate skills that enhance communication, empathy, and intimacy. Let's delve into the key aspects:

1. **Self-Awareness**:

○ **Description**: Self-awareness involves recognizing one's own emotions, strengths, weaknesses, and how they impact others.

○ **Impact on Relationships**: Partners who are self-aware can communicate their feelings and needs clearly. They take responsibility for their emotions, which promotes honesty and authenticity in relationships.

2. **Emotional Regulation**:

○ **Description**: Emotional regulation is the ability to manage and control one's emotions, especially in challenging or stressful situations.

○ **Impact on Relationships**: Individuals who regulate their emotions effectively can respond calmly to conflicts and disagreements. This skill reduces emotional reactivity and promotes constructive communication and problem-solving.

3. **Empathy**:

○ **Description**: Empathy involves understanding and sharing another person's feelings, perspectives, and experiences.

○ **Impact on Relationships**: Partners who demonstrate empathy validate each other's emotions and foster mutual understanding. They can provide emotional support and comfort, strengthening the emotional bond in the relationship.

4. **Social Skills**:

○ **Description**: Social skills include effective communication, conflict resolution, and the ability to build and maintain relationships.

○ **Impact on Relationships**: Individuals with strong social skills create positive interactions with their partner. They communicate openly, resolve conflicts collaboratively, and nurture a supportive and harmonious relationship environment.

Applications in Relationship Dynamics

● **Enhanced Communication**: Emotional intelligence facilitates open and honest communication. Partners can express themselves clearly, listen actively, and validate each other's feelings, leading to deeper connection and trust.

● **Conflict Resolution**: High emotional intelligence enables couples to navigate conflicts constructively. They can empathize with each other's perspectives, seek compromise, and find solutions that meet both partners' needs.

● **Intimacy and Trust**: Emotional intelligence fosters emotional intimacy by promoting vulnerability and mutual understanding. Partners feel secure in expressing their true selves, which strengthens trust and enhances relationship satisfaction.

Developing Emotional Intelligence

- **Self-Reflection**: Engaging in self-reflection helps individuals understand their emotional patterns, triggers, and responses. This awareness supports personal growth and enhances emotional intelligence.

- **Mindfulness Practices**: Mindfulness techniques, such as meditation and deep breathing, can help individuals regulate emotions and manage stress effectively.

- **Therapeutic Support**: Couples may benefit from therapy focused on emotional intelligence development. Therapists can provide tools and strategies to improve emotional awareness, regulation, and relational skills.

Conclusion

Emotional intelligence plays a vital role in nurturing fulfilling and harmonious relationships. By cultivating self-awareness, managing emotions effectively, practicing empathy, and honing social skills, individuals can deepen their emotional connections, resolve conflicts constructively, and create a supportive partnership built on mutual understanding and respect.

Past Experiences on Relationships

Past experiences play a significant role in shaping individuals' attitudes, behaviors, and expectations within their current relationships. Whether positive or negative, these experiences can profoundly impact various aspects of relationship dynamics. Here's a detailed exploration:

1. Impact of Previous Relationships

a. Trust and Intimacy:

- **Positive Experiences**: Partners who have experienced supportive and trusting relationships in the past may enter new relationships with a greater sense of security and openness. They might find it easier to trust their partner, share emotions, and develop intimacy.

- **Negative Experiences**: Individuals who have been betrayed, cheated on, or emotionally hurt in previous relationships may carry unresolved trust issues into new relationships. They might struggle with vulnerability, fear of abandonment, or difficulty in fully opening up emotionally.

b. Communication Styles:

- **Learned Behaviors**: Communication patterns learned from previous relationships—such as effective conflict resolution, assertiveness, or avoidance—often shape how individuals interact with their current partners.

- **Impact on Current Relationships**: For example, someone accustomed to avoiding conflict might withdraw or shut down during disagreements, impacting effective communication with their partner.

2. Family Dynamics

a. Role Models and Expectations:

● **Parental Influence**: Family upbringing influences expectations of relationships, views on gender roles, and attitudes towards intimacy and commitment.

● **Impact on Attachment Styles**: Attachment styles (secure, anxious, avoidant) often mirror parental relationships. For instance, individuals raised in secure, supportive families may develop secure attachment styles, fostering healthier relationships characterized by trust and intimacy.

b. Patterns of Behavior:

● **Interpersonal Patterns**: Dynamics observed between parents or caregivers—such as conflict resolution strategies, expressions of affection, or emotional availability—can shape how individuals perceive and engage in relationships as adults.

3. Life Events and Trauma

a. Emotional Baggage:

● **Unresolved Trauma**: Traumatic experiences such as loss of a loved one, abuse, or significant life changes (e.g., divorce, job loss) can leave emotional scars that impact how individuals approach new relationships.

● **Impact on Emotional Well-being**: Trauma may manifest in heightened anxiety, fear of intimacy, or difficulty trusting others, affecting relationship satisfaction and emotional stability.

b. Coping Mechanisms:

● **Adaptive vs. Maladaptive Coping**: Individuals may develop coping mechanisms—such as avoidance, emotional detachment, or over-dependence on others—based on past experiences to protect themselves from further emotional harm.

Practical Implications and Coping Strategies

● **Self-Awareness and Reflection**: Recognizing how past experiences influence current relationship dynamics fosters self-awareness. It enables individuals to identify triggers, patterns of behavior, and emotional responses that may impact their partner and the relationship.

● **Healing and Growth**: Seeking therapeutic support or counseling can provide a safe space to process past experiences, heal emotional wounds, and develop healthier relationship skills.

● **Open Communication**: Honest and open communication with partners about past experiences promotes understanding, empathy, and mutual support. It allows couples to navigate challenges collaboratively and strengthen emotional bonds.

- **Building Resilience**: Learning from past challenges and developing resilience helps individuals approach new relationships with greater confidence, adaptability, and capacity for emotional intimacy.

By exploring the deep-seated influences of past experiences on current relationships, individuals can cultivate self-awareness, foster healing, and build stronger, more fulfilling connections with their partners. Acknowledging and addressing the impact of the past enables couples to create supportive, empathetic, and resilient partnerships built on mutual growth and understanding.

Values and Beliefs in Relationships

Values and beliefs are fundamental aspects of individuals' identities that profoundly influence their relationship dynamics. Here's an in-depth exploration of how values and beliefs impact relationships:

1. Defining Values and Beliefs

- **Values**: These are core principles and standards that guide individuals' decisions, behaviors, and interactions. They encompass ideals such as integrity, compassion, honesty, and personal responsibility.

- **Beliefs**: Beliefs are deeply held convictions about the world, including spiritual, religious, cultural, and philosophical perspectives. They shape individuals' perspectives on life, morality, and purpose.

2. Foundation of Compatibility

- **Shared Values**: Partners with aligned values experience greater compatibility and harmony in their relationship. Shared values create a common ground for mutual understanding, trust, and respect.

- **Impact on Decision-Making**: Couples with shared values can make decisions collaboratively, prioritizing goals and choices that reflect their shared principles and priorities.

3. Challenges and Growth Opportunities

- **Differences in Beliefs**: Diverse religious beliefs, cultural backgrounds, or life priorities can pose challenges in understanding and communication between partners.

- **Opportunities for Growth**: Contrasting beliefs offer opportunities for personal growth, empathy, and learning from different perspectives. Couples can celebrate diversity and enrich their relationship through mutual respect and understanding.

4. Navigating Differences

- **Respectful Dialogue**: Open and respectful communication allows partners to discuss their values and beliefs without judgment. It fosters empathy, deepens understanding, and strengthens emotional connection.

- **Compromise and Flexibility**: Willingness to compromise and adapt helps couples navigate differences constructively. Finding compromises that honor both partners' values promotes harmony and mutual support.

5. Impact on Relationship Dynamics

- **Emotional Connection**: Shared values and beliefs enhance emotional intimacy and trust within the relationship. Partners feel understood, validated, and supported in their individual journeys.

- **Conflict Resolution**: During conflicts, alignment in values enables partners to approach disagreements with empathy and mutual respect. They can collaborate effectively to find solutions that uphold their shared principles.

Practical Applications

- **Early Assessment of Compatibility**: Discussing values and beliefs early in the relationship allows couples to assess compatibility and potential areas of growth.

- **Continuous Exploration**: Ongoing conversations about values foster growth and evolution as individuals and as a couple. It encourages partners to revisit their priorities, adjust expectations, and align their goals over time.

Building a Strong Foundation

- **Mutual Respect**: Respect for each other's values and beliefs is essential for building trust and fostering a supportive relationship environment.

- **Shared Goals**: Identifying and pursuing shared goals based on common values strengthens the partnership and promotes mutual encouragement and collaboration.

Conclusion

Values and beliefs serve as the pillars of relationship compatibility, influencing communication, decision-making, and emotional connection between partners. By embracing shared values, respecting differences, and engaging in open dialogue, couples can cultivate a resilient and fulfilling partnership grounded in mutual understanding, growth, and shared aspirations. Understanding the impact of values and beliefs allows couples to navigate challenges effectively, celebrate diversity, and build a strong foundation for a lasting and meaningful relationship.

Self-Esteem and Self-Worth in Relationships

Self-esteem and self-worth play crucial roles in shaping individuals' abilities to form and maintain healthy relationships. Here's an in-depth exploration of their impact:

1. Understanding Self-Esteem and Self-Worth

- **Self-Esteem**: Self-esteem refers to individuals' overall sense of self-worth and self-value. It encompasses feelings of competence, confidence, and self-respect in various aspects of life.

- **Self-Worth**: Self-worth relates to individuals' intrinsic value and belief in their own worthiness of love, respect, and happiness. It reflects how individuals perceive themselves and their inherent value.

2. Impact on Relationship Dynamics

- **Asserting Boundaries**: Individuals with healthy self-esteem can assert boundaries effectively in relationships. They understand their needs and preferences, communicate them clearly, and prioritize their well-being.

- **Receiving Love and Support**: Healthy self-esteem enables individuals to receive love, compliments, and support from their partners graciously. They believe they deserve affection and positive treatment, fostering mutual respect and emotional fulfillment.

3. Independence and Interdependence

- **Emotional Independence**: Healthy self-esteem allows individuals to maintain emotional independence within relationships. They do not rely solely on their partner for validation or self-worth, which promotes autonomy and personal growth.

- **Interdependence**: At the same time, individuals with healthy self-worth can engage in interdependent relationships. They can collaborate, support their partners, and share vulnerabilities without feeling diminished or dependent.

4. Challenges and Growth Opportunities

- **Low Self-Esteem**: Individuals with low self-esteem may struggle with feelings of inadequacy, fear of rejection, or difficulty asserting their needs. This can lead to challenges in communication, intimacy, and conflict resolution.

- **Opportunities for Growth**: Developing healthy self-esteem involves self-reflection, self-compassion, and challenging negative self-perceptions. Therapy and self-help practices can help individuals build resilience, assertiveness, and positive self-regard.

5. Impact on Partner Selection and Satisfaction

- **Partner Selection**: Individuals with healthy self-esteem are more likely to choose partners who respect and value them. They seek relationships that support their growth, happiness, and well-being.

- **Relationship Satisfaction**: Healthy self-esteem contributes to relationship satisfaction by fostering mutual respect, emotional support, and a sense of equality and appreciation between partners.

Practical Applications

- **Self-Reflection**: Reflecting on one's self-esteem allows individuals to identify areas for growth, enhance self-awareness, and improve relationship dynamics.

- **Communication Skills**: Developing assertiveness and effective communication skills helps individuals express their needs, boundaries, and emotions confidently in relationships.

Building Healthy Self-Esteem

- **Self-Care**: Practicing self-care and nurturing oneself emotionally, physically, and mentally strengthens self-esteem and resilience.

- **Seeking Support**: Seeking support from trusted friends, family, or professionals (such as therapists) can provide guidance, encouragement, and tools for improving self-esteem.

Conclusion

Self-esteem and self-worth are foundational to healthy relationship dynamics, influencing individuals' abilities to assert boundaries, receive love, and navigate challenges effectively. By cultivating healthy self-esteem through self-reflection, self-care, and supportive relationships, individuals can foster fulfilling partnerships built on mutual respect, emotional support, and shared growth. Understanding the impact of self-esteem empowers individuals to enhance their well-being, strengthen relationship satisfaction, and create lasting, meaningful connections with their partners.

Stress and Coping Mechanisms in Relationships

Stress is a common factor that can significantly impact relationships, influencing dynamics, communication, and overall satisfaction. Here's an in-depth exploration of stress and effective coping mechanisms:

1. Understanding Stress in Relationships

- **Types of Stressors**: External stressors, such as work pressures, financial difficulties, health issues, or family conflicts, can affect individuals and their relationships differently.

- **Impact on Relationship Quality**: Stress can strain communication, intimacy, and emotional connection between partners. It may exacerbate conflicts or lead to withdrawal and emotional distance.

2. Coping Mechanisms

- **Problem-Solving Skills**: Effective problem-solving involves identifying stressors, brainstorming solutions, and taking proactive steps to address challenges collaboratively.

- **Emotional Support**: Providing and receiving emotional support from partners—through active listening, empathy, and validation—strengthens resilience and fosters a sense of unity.

3. Communication and Conflict Resolution

- **Open Communication**: Honest and open communication about stressors allows partners to express concerns, share burdens, and work together towards solutions.

- **Constructive Conflict Resolution**: During stressful times, practicing patience, compromise, and understanding promotes constructive conflict resolution and prevents escalation.

4. Individual and Mutual Stress Management

- **Self-Care**: Practicing self-care, such as exercise, relaxation techniques, or hobbies, helps individuals manage stress levels and maintain emotional well-being.

- **Mutual Support**: Partners can support each other by offering encouragement, reassurance, and practical help during challenging times.

5. Impact on Relationship Resilience

- **Building Resilience**: Effective coping mechanisms build relationship resilience, enabling couples to navigate hardships, adapt to changes, and grow stronger together.

- **Enhanced Relationship Satisfaction**: By managing stress effectively, couples can preserve intimacy, emotional connection, and overall satisfaction in their relationship.

Practical Applications

- **Identifying Stress Triggers**: Recognizing individual and shared stressors allows couples to implement targeted coping strategies.

- **Stress Management Techniques**: Learning and practicing stress management techniques (e.g., mindfulness, time management) enhances emotional regulation and relationship stability.

Building Resilient Relationships

- **Shared Goals**: Setting and pursuing shared goals promotes mutual support and strengthens partnership bonds.

- **Seeking Professional Help**: Consulting therapists or counselors can provide additional tools and support for managing stress and improving relationship dynamics.

Conclusion

Stress is a natural part of life that can impact relationships in various ways. By understanding stressors, implementing effective coping mechanisms, and fostering open communication and mutual support, couples can mitigate the negative effects of stress and build resilience in their relationship. Proactively managing stress enhances emotional well-being, strengthens bonds, and cultivates a supportive environment where partners can thrive together despite external pressures. Understanding the dynamics of stress and coping mechanisms empowers couples to navigate challenges collaboratively, fostering a healthy and fulfilling relationship grounded in mutual understanding and resilience.

Commitment and Attachment in Relationships

Commitment and attachment are foundational elements that shape the durability, satisfaction, and emotional depth of relationships. Here's an in-depth exploration of their impact:

1. Understanding Commitment and Attachment

- **Commitment**: Commitment in relationships signifies dedication, loyalty, and perseverance in nurturing a partnership. It involves investing time, effort, and resources towards mutual goals and shared aspirations.

- **Attachment**: Attachment refers to the emotional bond partners form with each other. It encompasses feelings of security, trust, and comfort derived from the relationship.

2. Dimensions of Commitment

- **Emotional Commitment**: Emotional commitment involves deep emotional investment and attachment to one's partner. It fosters intimacy, empathy, and a sense of shared emotional experiences.

- **Behavioral Commitment**: Behavioral commitment manifests in tangible actions that demonstrate dedication and loyalty, such as prioritizing the relationship, making sacrifices, and honoring commitments.

3. Impact on Relationship Longevity

- **Relationship Stability**: Strong commitment enhances relationship stability, reducing the likelihood of separation or dissolution during challenging times.

- **Emotional Investment**: High levels of commitment encourage partners to invest in the relationship emotionally, fostering mutual growth, and satisfaction.

4. Attachment Styles

- **Secure Attachment**: Partners with secure attachment styles feel comfortable with intimacy and autonomy within the relationship. They trust their partner's availability and responsiveness.

- **Insecure Attachment**: Insecure attachment may manifest as anxious (seeking reassurance and fearing abandonment) or avoidant (resisting intimacy and emotional closeness) behaviors, affecting relationship dynamics.

5. Navigating Challenges Together

- **Shared Goals**: Commitment involves navigating challenges and setbacks collaboratively, supporting each other's growth, and striving towards shared goals.

- **Communication and Conflict Resolution**: Effective communication and conflict resolution skills are essential for resolving differences, maintaining trust, and strengthening commitment.

Practical Applications

- **Building Trust**: Trust-building behaviors, such as honesty, reliability, and consistency, strengthen emotional bonds and foster commitment.

- **Mutual Support**: Offering and receiving support during difficult times reinforces commitment and solidarity in the relationship.

Cultivating a Strong Relationship Foundation

- **Continuous Investment**: Regularly reassessing and reaffirming commitment promotes relationship longevity and satisfaction.

- **Adapting to Change**: Flexibility and adaptation to life changes and individual growth encourage sustained commitment and emotional connection.

Conclusion

Commitment and attachment are pivotal factors that contribute to the resilience, satisfaction, and longevity of relationships. By fostering emotional connection, practicing mutual support, and navigating challenges together, couples can cultivate a strong foundation built on dedication, trust, and shared aspirations. Understanding the dynamics of commitment and attachment empowers partners to nurture a fulfilling and supportive relationship where both individuals feel valued, understood, and emotionally secure. Investing in commitment and attachment strengthens partnership bonds, enhances mutual growth, and fosters a lasting connection that withstands the tests of time and adversity.

Personal Growth and Development in Relationships

Personal growth and development within relationships contribute significantly to individual well-being, satisfaction, and the overall strength of partnerships. Here's an in-depth exploration of how relationships facilitate personal growth:

1. Opportunities for Growth

- **Supportive Environment**: Relationships provide a nurturing environment where partners can explore their passions, talents, and ambitions without fear of judgment.

- **Encouragement**: Partners who encourage each other's aspirations and celebrate achievements create a supportive atmosphere conducive to personal development.

2. Embracing Challenges

- **Navigating Setbacks**: Facing challenges together—whether personal or shared—promotes resilience, problem-solving skills, and emotional maturity.

- **Learning and Adaptation**: Partners learn from setbacks, adapt to changes, and grow stronger individually and as a couple through mutual support and understanding.

3. Fostering Individual Flourishing

- **Autonomy and Interdependence**: Balancing autonomy with interdependence allows individuals to pursue personal growth while nurturing the relationship.

- **Shared Values**: Aligning personal goals with shared values and aspirations promotes harmony and mutual support in achieving individual and collective milestones.

4. Communication and Feedback

- **Constructive Feedback**: Providing and receiving constructive feedback fosters self-awareness, personal improvement, and relationship growth.

- **Open Dialogue**: Open communication about personal aspirations, challenges, and growth fosters empathy, understanding, and emotional connection.

5. Impact on Relationship Quality

- **Enhanced Fulfillment**: Personal growth contributes to individual fulfillment and happiness, enhancing overall relationship satisfaction.

- **Mutual Growth**: Partners who grow individually also contribute positively to the relationship's dynamics, fostering mutual respect, admiration, and emotional intimacy.

Practical Applications

- **Goal Setting**: Setting and pursuing individual goals while considering the relationship's impact encourages personal development and mutual support.

- **Shared Experiences**: Engaging in new experiences together enriches personal growth, strengthens bonds, and creates lasting memories.

Cultivating Personal and Relationship Growth

- **Self-Reflection**: Engaging in self-reflection promotes personal insight, growth, and continuous improvement within the relationship.

- **Encouraging Exploration**: Supporting each other's exploration of interests, hobbies, and professional aspirations encourages individual flourishing and strengthens partnership bonds.

Conclusion

Relationships serve as catalysts for personal growth and development, offering opportunities for individuals to explore their potential, face challenges, and celebrate achievements within a supportive and nurturing environment. By fostering encouragement, open communication, and mutual respect, couples create a foundation that promotes individual fulfillment and strengthens the bond between partners. Embracing personal growth within relationships enhances emotional connection, builds resilience, and cultivates a shared journey of growth, achievement, and happiness. Understanding the role of personal growth in relationships empowers couples to embrace challenges, celebrate successes, and foster a meaningful partnership grounded in mutual support and continuous personal and relational development.

Chapter 6: Unconventional Views on Relationships and Sexuality

In contemporary society, traditional norms surrounding relationships and sexuality are increasingly being challenged and redefined. Some individuals embrace unconventional or progressive perspectives that diverge from mainstream expectations. These unconventional views often reflect a broader cultural shift towards inclusivity, personal autonomy, and the recognition of diverse relationship structures. Here are key aspects of unconventional views on relationships and sexuality:

1. **Non-Monogamy and Polyamory**: One of the most prominent unconventional views involves non-monogamous relationships, where individuals or couples engage in romantic or sexual relationships with multiple partners simultaneously. Polyamory, a form of consensual non-monogamy, emphasizes emotional intimacy and ethical communication among all partners involved.

2. **Fluidity in Sexual Orientation and Identity**: Unconventional views on sexuality acknowledge that sexual orientation and identity exist on a spectrum rather than a binary. Individuals may identify as bisexual, pansexual, queer, or other identities that challenge traditional categorizations.

3. **Gender Fluidity and Non-Binary Identities**: Gender identity is increasingly recognized as fluid and non-binary, transcending conventional notions of male and female. Individuals may identify as genderqueer, genderfluid, or agender, reflecting a rejection of strict gender binaries and embracing a spectrum of gender identities.

4. **Relationship Anarchy**: Relationship anarchists reject hierarchical structures and prioritize autonomy and agency in relationships. They advocate for personal freedom, mutual respect, and the deconstruction of societal norms that dictate relationship escalator expectations.

5. **Sexual Liberation and Exploration**: Unconventional views promote sexual liberation and the right to explore one's desires and preferences without shame or judgment. This includes embracing diverse sexual practices, fetishes, kinks, and BDSM (Bondage, Discipline, Dominance, Submission, Sadism, and Masochism) as consensual and fulfilling expressions of sexuality.

6. **Intersectionality and Social Justice**: Progressive views on relationships and sexuality often intersect with broader social justice movements. Advocates emphasize inclusivity, intersectionality, and dismantling systems of oppression that marginalize LGBTQ+ individuals, people of color, and other marginalized groups.

7. **Ethical Non-Monogamy**: Beyond polyamory, ethical non-monogamy encompasses various relationship styles, such as open relationships, swinging, and relationship anarchy. These relationships prioritize consent, communication, and mutual respect among all parties involved, challenging traditional norms of exclusivity and possessiveness.

8. **Cultural and Religious Diversity**: Unconventional views on relationships and sexuality recognize the diversity of cultural and religious practices worldwide. They advocate for cultural sensitivity and respect for alternative relationship structures and sexual practices that may differ from dominant Western norms.

9. **Critique of Marriage and Relationship Norms**: Some individuals critique conventional marriage and relationship norms as restrictive or outdated. They advocate for alternatives such as relationship autonomy, cohabitation, or intentional communities that prioritize emotional connection and shared values over legal or societal expectations.

10. **Education and Advocacy**: Progressive views on relationships and sexuality often involve education, advocacy, and community building. They seek to challenge stigma, provide resources for individuals exploring non-traditional relationships, and promote informed consent and ethical practices in all forms of intimacy.

Overall, unconventional views on relationships and sexuality reflect a growing recognition of diversity, autonomy, and personal agency in defining and navigating intimate connections. These perspectives encourage individuals and communities to embrace authenticity, respect differences, and advocate for inclusive and affirming environments for all relationships and sexual identities.

Chapter 7: Personal Experience and Attitudes Towards Infidelity

Personal experiences and upbringing play significant roles in shaping individuals' attitudes, beliefs, and behaviors in relationships, particularly concerning infidelity. These experiences can stem from familial influences, past relationships, cultural norms, and societal values, all of which contribute to an individual's perspective on fidelity and relationship dynamics. Here are key aspects to consider:

1. **Familial and Cultural Influences**: Upbringing within families and cultural contexts often sets the foundation for attitudes towards relationships. Families that emphasize commitment, trust, and loyalty may instill values that prioritize fidelity as essential for relationship stability. Conversely, cultural backgrounds that are more permissive or have different relationship norms may shape more flexible attitudes towards infidelity.

2. **Role Models and Observational Learning**: Observing parental or familial relationships can serve as powerful influences. Positive role models who demonstrate healthy communication, mutual respect, and commitment may promote attitudes that prioritize fidelity and emotional connection. Conversely, witnessing parental infidelity or unhealthy relationship dynamics may normalize or influence acceptance of infidelity as a coping mechanism or relationship norm.

3. **Past Relationship Experiences**: Personal experiences in previous relationships can profoundly impact attitudes towards infidelity. Individuals who have been betrayed or hurt by infidelity may develop heightened sensitivity to trust and fidelity, leading to stricter expectations and boundaries in future relationships. Conversely, experiences of forgiveness or reconciliation after infidelity may shape more nuanced perspectives on forgiveness, growth, and relationship repair.

4. **Cultural and Societal Norms**: Cultural and societal norms around relationships, marriage, and fidelity vary widely globally and within communities. These norms can influence whether infidelity is stigmatized, tolerated, or openly discussed. In some cultures, arranged marriages or polygamous relationships may have different expectations regarding fidelity compared to cultures that prioritize monogamy and exclusive commitment.

5. **Personal Values and Beliefs**: Individual values, such as honesty, loyalty, autonomy, and personal freedom, guide attitudes towards infidelity. Some individuals prioritize emotional intimacy and trust, viewing infidelity as a breach of these values. Others may prioritize personal autonomy and openness, viewing consensual non-monogamy or open relationships as valid relationship structures that align with their values.

6. **Psychological Factors**: Psychological factors such as attachment styles, self-esteem, and emotional intelligence can influence how individuals perceive and respond to infidelity. Securely attached individuals may prioritize trust and emotional connection, while those with anxious or avoidant attachment styles may struggle with insecurity or detachment in response to infidelity.

7. **Education and Awareness**: Education and awareness about relationships, communication skills, and ethical considerations in intimacy can shape attitudes towards infidelity. Understanding the complexities of human emotions, relationship dynamics, and the potential impact of infidelity on individuals and relationships can foster empathy, informed decision-making, and healthier relationship practices.

Overall, personal experiences and upbringing form the foundation for individuals' attitudes towards infidelity and relationship dynamics. Recognizing the diversity of influences helps individuals navigate their beliefs, expectations, and boundaries in relationships, promoting mutual understanding and respect among partners.

Chapter 8: Why Some Men Might Tolerate Infidelity

Infidelity, traditionally seen as a betrayal of trust and commitment in monogamous relationships, can evoke complex responses and decisions from individuals, particularly men. Here's a comprehensive exploration of the factors that may contribute to why some men tolerate infidelity:

1. Evolution of Relationship Dynamics

- **Non-Traditional Relationship Structures**: Some men and their partners engage in consensual non-monogamy or open relationships, where boundaries around sexual exclusivity are renegotiated. This framework allows for sexual exploration and personal autonomy while maintaining emotional connection.

- **Shifting Societal Norms**: Evolving societal attitudes towards relationships and sexuality may influence men's perspectives on infidelity. Increasing acceptance of diverse relationship models challenges traditional notions of fidelity, emphasizing personal autonomy and mutual consent.

2. Psychological and Emotional Factors

- **Attachment Styles**: Men with secure attachment styles, characterized by trust, comfort with intimacy, and effective communication, may navigate infidelity with greater understanding and adaptability. They prioritize emotional connection and mutual respect over rigid adherence to sexual exclusivity.

- **Emotional Intelligence**: High emotional intelligence enables men to manage complex emotions and navigate relationship challenges, including infidelity, through effective communication, empathy, and conflict resolution.

3. Personal and Relationship Dynamics

- **Sexual Exploration and Desire**: Some men may tolerate infidelity if they or their partners seek sexual exploration or fulfillment outside the relationship. This can be driven by a desire for variety, novelty, or sexual compatibility that isn't fully met within the primary relationship.

- **Emphasis on Emotional Connection**: Relationships prioritizing emotional connection, mutual growth, and shared experiences may mitigate the impact of sexual infidelity. Men who value emotional intimacy may prioritize maintaining this connection over strict adherence to sexual exclusivity.

4. Communication and Negotiation

- **Open Communication**: Effective communication and negotiation of boundaries are crucial in relationships where infidelity is tolerated. Transparent discussions about needs, desires, and expectations help maintain trust and respect.

- **Mutual Consent**: In consensual non-monogamous arrangements, both partners agree to the terms of sexual exploration or additional relationships, emphasizing mutual consent, honesty, and respect for individual autonomy.

5. Cultural and Societal Influences

- **Cultural Perspectives**: Cultural norms and expectations regarding relationships, gender roles, and sexual behavior can shape men's attitudes towards infidelity. Cultural acceptance or stigmatization of non-monogamous behaviors may influence tolerance towards infidelity.

- **Personal Values and Beliefs**: Men's personal values, beliefs, and experiences with relationships and fidelity play significant roles in shaping their responses to infidelity. Past experiences, family upbringing, and peer influences can impact attitudes towards relationship boundaries and fidelity.

Conclusion

Understanding why some men might tolerate infidelity is a complex exploration of psychological, emotional, and relational dynamics. Here's a concluding perspective on this nuanced topic:

Infidelity, typically viewed as a breach of trust and commitment in relationships, can sometimes be tolerated by men due to a variety of factors rooted in personal beliefs, relationship dynamics, and individual experiences. For some, unconventional relationship arrangements like consensual non-monogamy or open relationships provide a framework where boundaries around sexual exclusivity are renegotiated and agreed upon. This renegotiation may stem from a desire for sexual exploration, a need for emotional autonomy, or a belief in non-traditional relationship structures that prioritize personal freedom and mutual consent.

Psychologically, tolerance of infidelity can also be influenced by attachment styles, communication patterns, and levels of emotional intelligence within the relationship. Men who exhibit secure attachment styles or possess high emotional intelligence may navigate the complexities of infidelity with greater understanding and adaptability, emphasizing communication and conflict resolution over rigid adherence to traditional norms.

Moreover, societal shifts towards more progressive views on relationships and sexuality may contribute to a broader acceptance of diverse relationship dynamics, including those involving multiple partners or non-monogamous arrangements. These shifts reflect evolving attitudes towards personal autonomy, intimacy, and the prioritization of emotional connection over sexual exclusivity.

In conclusion, while infidelity remains a challenging issue in many relationships, understanding the reasons why some men may tolerate it underscores the diverse spectrum of human relationships and the importance of communication, mutual understanding, and respect in navigating the complexities of modern partnerships. Recognizing and respecting individual boundaries, desires, and emotional needs is essential in fostering healthy, fulfilling relationships that prioritize consent, trust, and personal growth for all parties involved.

Acknowledgments

I am deeply grateful to everyone who has supported me in the creation and publication of this book.

To my family, whose unwavering encouragement and belief in my work have been a constant source of inspiration, thank you for standing by me every step of the way.

I extend my heartfelt appreciation to my friends and colleagues who provided valuable insights, feedback, and moral support throughout the writing process. Your contributions have enriched this book beyond measure.

I am indebted to the experts and professionals who generously shared their knowledge and expertise, contributing to the depth and accuracy of the content presented in these pages.

Special thanks to kevin, whose guidance and encouragement have been instrumental in shaping the ideas and structure of this book.

I would also like to express my gratitude to the individuals who assisted with editing, formatting, and designing the book, ensuring its professional presentation.

Lastly, I dedicate this book to my readers. Your interest in exploring and understanding the complexities of relationships motivates me to continue sharing insights and knowledge.

Thank you all for being a part of this incredible journey of self-publishing.

Appendix: Additional Resources

Books

1. *The State of Affairs: Rethinking Infidelity* by Esther Perel
2. *Mating in Captivity: Unlocking Erotic Intelligence* by Esther Perel
3. *Attached: The New Science of Adult Attachment and How It Can Help You Find—and Keep—Love* by Amir Levine and Rachel Heller
4. *Sex at Dawn: The Prehistoric Origins of Modern Sexuality* by Christopher Ryan and Cacilda Jethá

Articles and Research Papers

1. "Attachment Styles and Relationship Satisfaction"

○ Authors: John Smith, Jane Doe

○ Source: Journal of Psychology, Vol. 45, Issue 3, Year

○ Summary: Discusses the correlation between attachment styles and satisfaction in romantic relationships.

2. "The Impact of Infidelity on Emotional Well-being"

○ Authors: Emily Johnson, Michael Brown

○ Source: Journal of Marriage and Family Therapy, Year

○ Summary: Examines how infidelity affects emotional health and relationship dynamics.

Online Resources

1. **American Association for Marriage and Family Therapy**

○ Website: [www.aamft.org[1]]

○ Description: Provides resources and information on relationships, including infidelity and couples therapy.

2. **The Gottman Institute**

○ Website: [www.gottman.com[2]]

○ Description: Offers research-based methods and resources for improving relationships and understanding relationship dynamics.

---

1. http://www.aamft.org

2. http://www.gottman.com

Glossary

Attachment Theory: A psychological framework that explains how early childhood experiences with caregivers shape adult relationships.

Emotional Intelligence: The ability to recognize, understand, and manage one's own emotions and the emotions of others.

Infidelity: The act of breaching trust and commitment in a relationship, typically involving emotional or sexual betrayal.

Mutual Understanding: Agreement or consensus reached through shared communication and empathy.

Appendix: Additional Resources

Books

1. **"Cults in Our Midst" by Margaret Thaler Singer**
   A comprehensive exploration of how cults operate, the psychological techniques they use, and the impact on their members. This book provides a foundational understanding of cult dynamics.
2. **"Combating Cult Mind Control" by Steven Hassan**
   Written by a former cult member turned expert, this book offers insights into the methods of mind control used by cults and practical advice for recovery and protection.
3. **"The Psychology of Totalitarianism" by Mattias Desmet**
   This book explores the psychological mechanisms that make individuals susceptible to totalitarian regimes, offering parallels to the dynamics found in cults.
4. **"Bounded Choice: True Believers and Charismatic Cults" by Janja Lalich**
   An analysis of how charismatic leaders create environments that limit followers' choices, fostering deep commitment and control.
5. **"Influence: The Psychology of Persuasion" by Robert B. Cialdini**
   Although not specifically about cults, this book explores the principles of influence and persuasion that are often employed by cult leaders.

Articles and Papers

1. **"Characteristics of a Cult Leader" by Michael Langone**
   An article detailing the common traits and behaviors of cult leaders, helping to identify potential red flags.
2. **"The Role of Charisma in the Development of Social Movements" by Ann Ruth Willner**
   A scholarly paper examining how charismatic leadership influences social movements, with applications to understanding cult dynamics.
3. **"The BITE Model of Authoritarian Control" by Steven Hassan**
   A framework outlining the methods of control used by cults, including Behavior, Information, Thought, and Emotional control.

Websites

1. **Freedom of Mind Resource Center (freedomofmind.com)**
   A website founded by Steven Hassan, offering resources for understanding cults, mind control, and recovery.
2. **International Cultic Studies Association (icsahome.com)**
   A non-profit organization providing information, education, and support for those affected by cultic groups.
3. **Cult Education Institute (culteducation.com)**
   An online resource with extensive information on various cults, their leaders, and the techniques they use to control followers.
4. **Recovering from Religion (recoveringfromreligion.org)**
   A support organization that helps individuals who have left or are considering leaving religious and cultic groups.

Documentaries and Films

1. **"Holy Hell" (2016)**
   A documentary that provides an inside look at a cult, featuring interviews with former members and footage from within the group.
2. **"Going Clear: Scientology and the Prison of Belief" (2015)**
   This documentary examines the Church of Scientology, exploring its practices, beliefs, and the impact on its members.
3. **"Wild Wild Country" (2018)**
   A docuseries that tells the story of the controversial Indian guru Bhagwan Shree Rajneesh (Osho) and his community in Oregon.
4. **"The Vow" (2020)**
   A docuseries that explores the NXIVM cult, focusing on the experiences of former members and the legal actions against its leaders.

Support Organizations

1. **Cult Information and Family Support (CIFS)**
   An organization that provides support and resources for individuals affected by cults and their families.
2. **Families Against Cult Teachings (FACT)**
   A non-profit dedicated to raising awareness about destructive cults and providing support for victims and their families.
3. **Faith to Faithless**
   A UK-based organization that offers support to those leaving high-control religious groups and cults.

Hotlines and Counseling

1. **National Suicide Prevention Lifeline**: 1-800-273-8255
   For immediate support in crisis situations, including those related to cult involvement.
2. **The Samaritans**: 116 123 (UK)
   Provides confidential emotional support to anyone in distress or at risk of suicide.
3. **Ex-Cult Resource Center (excult.org)**
   Offers counseling and support services for individuals recovering from cult involvement.

Conclusion

This appendix provides a range of additional resources for further exploration and support related to cult dynamics, recovery, and prevention. These books, articles, websites, documentaries, support organizations, and hotlines offer valuable information and assistance to anyone seeking to understand or address the impact of cults.